THE
DEVIL'S ATLAS

Detail of the title page of Alexandre Perier's Desenganno dos Peccadores *('Disillusion of Sinners', 1724), engraved by GFL Debrie.*

THE
DEVIL'S ATLAS

An Explorer's Guide to Heavens,
Hells and Afterworlds

EDWARD
BROOKE-HITCHING

SIMON &
SCHUSTER

London · New York · Sydney · Toronto · New Delhi

MMXXI

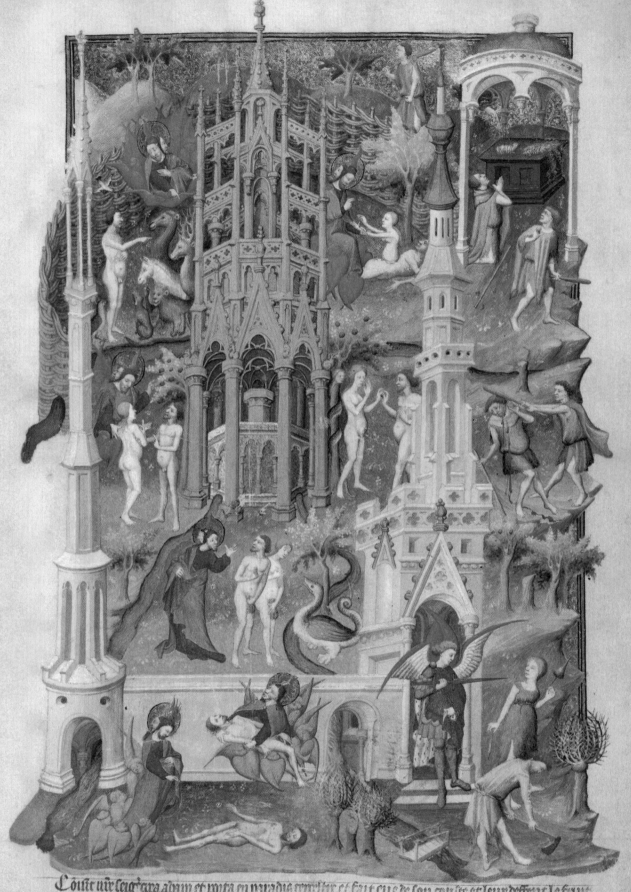

Cõmt̃e uir̃ seig̃ a̓ra adam et p̃oita en p̃aradis ŧeŗŗn̄e et fait eue de son coste et leur defent le fru̇t

To Franklin and Emma

'For they shall be an ornament
of grace unto thy head'
Proverbs 1:8-9

CONTENTS

INTRODUCTION 8

PART ONE: HELLS AND
UNDERWORLDS 18
The Ancient Egyptian Duat 20
The Kur Netherworld of Ancient
   Mesopotamia 24
Zoroastrian Afterworlds: The House
   of Lies and the House of Song 28
The Hells of Ancient India 32
Hells of the East 40
Hades 50
Hel: The Norse Underworld 56
Jahannam: Islamic Hell 60
Mesoamerican Underworlds 68
Biblical Hell 74
   Sheol and Gehenna 74
   Visions and Tours of Hell 84
   Into the Hell-Mouth 91
   A Brief History of the Devil 92
   Dante's *Inferno* and the Mapping
      of Hell 104
   The Evolution of Hell 116

PART TWO: LIMBO, PURGATORY
AND OTHER MIDWORLDS 132
Midworlds 132
Limbo 136
Purgatory 140

PART THREE: HEAVENS,
PARADISES AND UTOPIAS 148
A'aru of Ancient Egypt 150
Heavens of Ancient India 154
Heavens of the East 162
Greece and Rome: The Golden Age,
   the Elysian Fields and the Islands
   of the Blessed 168
Mesoamerican Heavens 174
Jannah: The Islamic Garden Paradise 184
Valhalla 190
Biblical Heaven 194
Mapping the Garden of Eden 218
Thomas More's *Utopia* 226
The Edible Paradise of Cockaigne 230
Dowie's Zion 238

CONCLUSION 242

SELECT BIBLIOGRAPHY 246

INDEX 248

ACKNOWLEDGEMENTS
AND PICTURE CREDITS 254

OPPOSITE: *Death's coat of arms,
from an early sixteenth-century
German heraldry manuscript.*

INTRODUCTION

'We take death to reach a star.'
Vincent van Gogh

In the year of our Lord 2019, on the thirty-first day of January, an extraordinary event occurred. You'd be forgiven for having missed it, what with the day's headlines reporting wildfires raging across Tasmania; a 73-year-old French yachtsman named Jean-Luc Van Den Heede winning a round-the-world solo race without instruments; and MIT researchers announcing their invention of a robot that had mastered the game of Jenga (*finally*, I hear you cry). But there it was, marked in official meteorological records: Hell had frozen over. Literally. The temperature in Hell plummeted to a record low of –26°C (–14.8°F), a depth of cold not experienced there for over a century. For the inhabitants of Hell, a small unincorporated community in Livingston County, Michigan, USA (population about eighty or so, town slogan 'Go to Hell!'), the polar vortex that struck their homes was little more than an inconvenience, and not nearly as irritating as the national newspapers cackling over the irony.[1]

For as long as we've lived in this world, we've been obsessed with the next. The idea for this book came about in 2011, when in the basement of a small London rare book shop I chanced upon a folded wad of rag paper, inauspiciously torn at the creases and heavily foxed. Opening it up to its full size, however, was a revelation. Entitled *La carte du royaume des cieux, avec le chemin pour y aller* (Map of the Kingdom of Heaven, With the Way to Get There), here was a vast, detailed map of heaven, purgatory and hell together in one grand design, an exhortatory broadside made to be pasted up around the streets of Paris *c.*1650

---

1 There are two competing stories as to the origin of the naming of the town of Hell. The first is that on one dazzlingly sunny afternoon sometime in the 1830s a newly arrived German traveller stepped down from his stagecoach, squinted in the sunshine and remarked to his companion *So schön hell!* (How beautifully bright!) This was overheard by a local, and the name stuck. To be honest I much prefer the second explanation: the town's original settler, George Reeves, was asked for his thoughts on what the place should be called. Reeves reflected on the swarms of mosquitos, impenetrably thick forests, treacherous wetlands and other torturous local features that had greeted him on his arrival, and replied: 'I don't give a shit. You can name it Hell for all I care.' And lo, on 13 October 1841, the town of Hell was officially christened.

A torture of Zoroastrian hell, from a c.1589 copy of the prophet Zarathustra's Book of Ardā Wīrāz

(see page 195 for this map). In no less than majestic fashion, its author had captured the nebulous geography and architecture of the unseen with solid lines and measured, geographical space. Drinking in the map brought the realisation of the phenomenal rarity of such an object. Not just its form – surviving examples of any such disposable street materials are of course exceedingly rare – but in its theme. Hells like the aforementioned of Livingston County, and indeed towns named Heaven, Paradise and other afterworld-inspired toponyms, litter maps of the globe.[2] But how often has the attempt been made to map their metaphysical inspirations?

This sparked an obsessive quest to track down works created around the world, across the ages, to chart, depict and describe the afterlife. Over a period of nearly ten years a

---

2 See also the Norwegian village of Hell, where tourists take selfies in front of the Hell railway station sign, which reads *Gods-Expedition* – archaic Norwegian for 'freight service'; and whence came Miss Mona Grudt, a Norwegian beauty contestant who lent a metaphysical quality to the 1990 Miss Universe competition title when she advertised herself as 'The beauty queen from Hell'.

deathly collection began to form, culled from the archives of libraries, private collections and further lucky discoveries in dealers' premises around the world. A rummage in an antiques store in Brittany, France, for example, turned up a truly jaw-dropping, sixteenth-century parchment painting of the Zoroastrian hell and paradise with a unique diagonal division (see page 28). A visit to a Polish dealer led to the discovery of a purported late-eighteenth-century portrait of a decidedly cheeky Antichrist (see page 103). A search in Madrid yielded a mesmerising hieroglyphic letter from the Devil; and so on.

This inspired journeys to other European cities to visit the great divine and infernal church-wall frescoes and celebrated Renaissance masterworks, as well as pilgrimages to find the medieval 'doom murals' hidden in churches throughout the United Kingdom, like the 17ft- (5.2m-) wide example in Chaldon, Surrey (see page 85). This book is the result of those years of searching.

This is an atlas of the afterlife; a guide to the landscapes of the 'undiscovered country from whose bourn no traveler returns', as Shakespeare describes it in *Hamlet* (Act 3, Scene 1). Here are the cities, mountains, palaces, underworlds, torture chambers, drinking halls, demonic parliaments, golden fields, rivers of blood and lakes of fire that make up the geographies of death of religions and cultures around the world. What are these places actually like, and who will we find there?

The Devil's Atlas charts the various ways in which scholars, artists and cartographers across the centuries have risen to the paradoxical challenge of these questions, with the certain knowledge that the answers are beyond human reach. This is a book about mapping the unmappable and painting the indescribable, to explore the unexplorable. To be clear, this is not a history of world religion, nor a journey focused on the how, or the why; but specifically the *where*, intended to be read in a spirit of universal interest, as insight into the historical imagination in engagement with the continually discomforting subject of mortality.

Physical descriptions of these otherworlds are collected from the earliest and most revered sources like the Judaeo-Christian Scriptures, the Qur'an and Islamic Hadiths, as well as more esoteric works like apocalyptic testimonies, divine revelations and colourful outsider theories. Each realm is accompanied with cartographic and artistic representations inspired by these

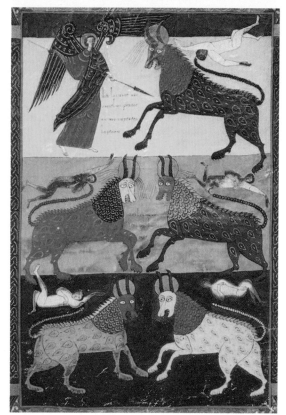

original descriptions through the ages. As such, this book also operates as a field manual of sorts for the afterlife explorer, examining the reported celestial flora, fauna and other sights, smells and sounds of these realms, along with the variety of deific and demonic figures that one might encounter in these spiritual landscapes.

What is of particular interest are the practical efforts to apply earthly metrics to these intangible realms. Often this can be with time. The date of 13 February is marked in a number of medieval calendars of Christendom as the day on which hell was created. In Hinduism, the entire length of existence of the universe is a single reverie of the god Brahma in just one day of his time – for us, the daydream lasts for about 34 billion years. Then night falls for Brahma, the universe fades and the next day he dreams anew. This is reminiscent of Ash'ari theology advocated by some Muslim philosophers, which states that Allah is continually destroying and recreating the universe at every moment. (Which is similar, too, curiously enough, to the modern quantum field theory that argues that our existence involves us being annihilated and reformed many times per second.)

The populace of heaven and hell has always been another theme of intellectual interrogation. In the late seventeenth century, the theologian Thomas Burnet deduced that, since

ABOVE LEFT: *'The Dragon gives his power to the Beast'.* ABOVE RIGHT: *'The fifth trumpet, the locusts transform into horses'. Both from Beatus of Liébana's* Commentary on the Apocalypse, *eighth century.*

FOLLOWING PAGES: The Temptation of St Anthony *(c.1650) by the Flemish painter Joos van Craesbeeck. St Anthony sits, plagued by demons, amid a hellscape of van Craesbeeck's imagining (the large head in the centre is the artist's own).*

there would be political government in heaven, it would have to be divided into nations. The English, French, Germans and Italians would therefore have to be kept separated 'in the air'. Many analysed references in the final book of the Bible, Revelation, to calculate the demonic population and hierarchy of hell. The medieval mathematician Michael Scot (1175-*c.*1232) concluded there to be 14,198,580 demons; the Spanish Bishop Alphonsus de Spina (*fl.* 1491) inflated that estimate to 133,306,668 and published his own classification of demons, as did many authors including King James VI in 1591. Particularly notorious is the hierarchy in the *Dictionnaire infernal* (1818) by Jacques Collin de Plancy, which was republished in 1863 with sixty-nine portraits of various demons. It is here, for example, that we learn of the political positions in hell, with descriptions of demons like Adramelech, 'king of fire', eighth of the ten arch-demons, and grand chancellor of hell.

The Franciscan friar Berthold of Regensburg (*c.*1210-72) believed only one in 100,000 people would be allowed into heaven; which would certainly fit with the relatively modest proportions of the Christian heaven described in Chapter 21 of Revelation. Here, heaven is a symmetrical cube 12,000 furlongs on each side. One furlong is one-eighth of a mile, which means heaven is 1500 miles (2414km) on each side. If it came to rest on Earth, heaven would therefore cover a land mass equal to about one-half of the United States. In contrast, Vaikuntha, the heaven of the Hindu god Vishnu, is 80,000 miles (128,750km) in circumference. Elsewhere, the Sanskrit epic *Mahabharata* reveals that the heaven of the god Brahma is 800 miles (1288km) long, 400 miles (644km) wide and 40 miles (64km) high.

And what of the proportions of God Himself? In the *Sefer Raziel HaMalakh*, a thirteenth-century grimoire of Practical Kabbalah purportedly written by the angel Raziel, it is divulged that the Jewish god is 2,300,000,000 *parasangs* high, or 7.2 billion miles (11.6 billion km) (for comparison, this is more than twice the current distance of Pluto from the Earth). From the *Saundarya Lahari*, a Hindu text thought to have been written on the mystical Mount Meru, we learn that the entire cosmos is but a mote of dust on the foot of the all-encompassing female deity Mahadevi. And in the revered Hindu text *Bhagavata Purana*, this mind-boggling cosmic scale is brought back to us, full circle, with the poetic

Top: *Adramelech, grand chancellor of hell. From the 1863 illustrated edition of the* Dictionnaire Infernal. Above: *Bael, first king of hell, from the same work.*

statement: 'There are innumerable universes besides this one, and although they are unlimitedly large, they move about like atoms in you. Therefore you are called unlimited.'

Cartographically, an empirical approach towards the immeasurable is at the heart of the Renaissance obsession with 'infernal cartography', the challenge to precisely map the hell of Dante's *Inferno* (see page 108), the definitive work in the construction of the Western European image of hell. What with hell being so deep beneath the surface of the Earth, none could argue with those charting the Italian poet's conical netherworld. This was not a luxury that could be enjoyed by those map-makers attempting to pinpoint the location of the Earthly Paradise (see page 224), as they became caught in the transitional phase of cartography from allegorical mapping to the newly rediscovered Ptolemaic system of coordinates, which stretched landmasses on maps into their first accurate shapes with mathematical methodology. Suddenly, a map was required to have practical geographical accuracy, so where to mark traditional belief features like the Garden of Eden?

This puzzle of fitting both heaven and hell in the material universe continued through the Age of Enlightenment, with outside-the-box thinkers like Tobias Swinden (see page 121) and his extra-terrestrial relocation of hell in his *Enquiry Into the Nature and Place of Hell* (1714), devising solutions as brilliant in their simplicity as they are mind-boggling in their strangeness. It's a tradition that continues to this day, albeit on the fringes of coherence. Particularly intriguing are the broadcasts of the American televangelist Dr Jack Van Impe (1931-2020) of Jack Van Impe Ministries, who in 2001 declared that black holes fit all the technical requirements to be the location of hell. (Van Impe caused a similar stir again in 2007, with the announcement that the basic design of the automobile could be found in the Bible.)

So where do heaven and hell sit today in popular preoccupation? A 2017 UK Religion Survey conducted on behalf of the BBC found that 46 per cent of people believe in some form of life after death; of those, 65 per cent believed this to be a heaven or hell. Meanwhile, in America, belief in Satan is apparently on the rise: according to Gallup polls across recent decades, 55 per cent of Americans said they believed in the Devil in 1990 – in 2001, this was 68 per cent, and by 2007 it had increased to 70 per cent. Separately, a 2011 Associated Press –

A legendary tree of the Chilean island of Chiloé, which was reported to grow in the shape of Jesus on the Cross. From Descripción historial archipielago de Chiloé *(1791) by Father Pedro Gonzalez de Agüeros.*

The Soul of Man. XLIII. *Anima hominis*,

GfK poll showed that 77 per cent of adult Americans believe in angels. And in 1997, a US News & World Report poll asked 1000 Americans who was 'somewhat likely' to go to heaven: Bill Clinton scored 52 per cent, Princess Diana 60 per cent and Mother Theresa came in second with 79 per cent. In first place, though, with 87 per cent, were the respondents to the poll, who gave themselves top marks.

However much the vibrancy of heavens and hells varies in modern popular belief, there remains a universally instinctive fascination with the mystery of what will come. Ultimately, what makes the descriptions, maps, paintings and other material traces of afterworlds collected in this book so endlessly fascinating is that they are attempts at achieving the impossible. Indeed, the term *ineffabilis* ('too great to be expressed in words') was introduced to theology in the fifth century by St Augustine (354-430), who explained that it is easier to describe what God and heaven is not, than to say what He, and it, is. The world that awaits is simply beyond the descriptive power of human language. This he drew from Paul's statement to the Corinthians: 'Eye has not seen, nor ear heard the things that God has prepared for those who love him' (1 Corinthians 2:9). Nevertheless, here are the results of millennia of human endeavour to unravel that mystery.

'The Soul of Man', from the 1705 English edition of The World of Things Obvious to the Senses, *the first picture book made for the education of young children.*

Opposite: *Albrecht Dürer's 1498 woodcut print of the Four Horsemen of the Apocalypse.*

HELLS AND UN

Welcome to hell. Or, in the words glimpsed by Dante as he passes through the gates to the Inferno: 'Abandon all hope, ye who enter here.' It was this imagery that inspired Auguste Rodin to conceive his famous sculpture *The Gates of Hell*, an infernal doorway through which the imagination of the viewer was invited to wander. Historically, there have been a number of 'true' (certainly truly feared) earthly portals to the hells and underworlds of various faiths.

While the entry requirement of expiration is invariably the same (though not always a hard-and-fast rule, as we shall see), numerous features of real-world geography have played the part of nexus between earthly and spiritual realms. To reach the Hades of antiquity, Kingdom of the Shades, one can follow in the footsteps of Orpheus and Hercules and visit the Cape Matapan Caves on the southernmost point of the Greek mainland; or the Necromanteion of Ephyra at Mesopotamos. Volcanoes too have long been associated with entrances to the fiery underworld – the Icelandic stratovolcano Hekla was feared in Christian tradition as the egress to Satan's fiery pit. In China, a look at hell can be found in municipal form at Fengdu, 'City of Ghosts', where landmarks include Ghost Torturing Pass and Last Glance at Home Tower, and where statues of demons performing their daily tortures can be found around the town.

But what exactly are the workings of these realms of which these portals offer mere glimpses? Any exploration of global afterworld belief must launch in Africa, specifically with the ancient culture possessing the most ornate death-worship practices and elaborately imaginative post-death worlds to have ever ignited the minds of men.

BACKGROUND IMAGE:
A demonic float that formed part of the enormous procession organised at Dresden for the pleasure of Augustus II in 1695.

DERWORLDS

The Gates of Hell *by Auguste Rodin, who spent thirty-seven years crafting the sculpture from a scene from Dante's* Inferno *until his death in 1917. Museo Soumaya, Mexico City.*

THE ANCIENT EGYPTIAN DUAT

When we think of the ancient Egyptians, we think of death. This is because of what has survived of their culture, which arguably more than any other obsessed and luxuriated in the ritualised treatment of their dead. The buildings of everyday Egyptian life made from reeds, wood and mud bricks have long since perished; but the stone pyramid tombs of the pharaohs have resisted the violence of millennia to define our image of their ancient creators. Mummified corpses, their preservation considered essential for a contented afterlife, still lurch their way around modern popular culture. The most famous relics called to mind when speaking of ancient Egypt are all funereal in purpose. The pyramid tombs of the ancient pharaohs and their various burial contents all served some use in either ushering one to, or helping one prosper in, the Duat (underworld).

One of the most commonly uncovered types of artefact, the *ushabti* figurine, was designed for just this purpose. The doll-like figures (see example shown on page 22) were usually inscribed with the sixth-chapter text of the infamous *Book of the Dead* (the original title of which more accurately translates to the chirpier 'Book of Emerging Forth into the Light'), a funerary text of magic spells compiled by numerous priests across 1000 years to assist the deceased's journey through the Duat. The figurines were scattered among the other goods in the grave to operate as assistants to the deceased in the next life. (Inscriptions on their legs announced their cheerful readiness to perform this servile task.) The abundance of *ushabti* is closely followed by that of scarabs, the beetle-shaped amulets and administrative seals that, by the early New Kingdom, were copiously deployed as part of the ritual protection items guarding a mummy in its tomb.

The ultimate goal of the deceased Egyptian was to reach the blissful Kingdom of Osiris and the heavenly A'aru, or the 'Fields of Rushes' (see page 150), the reward for terrestrially well-behaved souls. Decorative scenes of this lush place were carved and painted hopefully on the walls of tombs, such as that of Menna, an inspector of royal estates buried in the Valley of the Nobles, near Luxor. (Fret not, potential resident of noble blood, the luxurious fields of wheat will be worked for you by

ABOVE: *A detail from the* Book of the Dead *of the Theban scribe Ani, created c.1250 BC, depicting the human-headed, bird-bodied ba of the deceased, one of the imagined forms of the human soul.*

BELOW: *An ancient Egyptian papyrus depicting the journey into the afterlife. Officially entitled* Guide to the Afterlife for the Custodian of the Property of the Amon Temple Amonemwidja with Symbolic Illustrations Concerning the Dangers in the Netherworld.

the *ushabti* helpers.) But to reach this paradise, the deceased have to journey through the hellish Duat underworld until they reach the grand Hall of Ma'at for 'the weighing of the heart', a judgement performed by the dog-headed god Anubis, under the watchful gaze of Osiris, king of the underworld.

It is crucial to follow every instruction provided in the *Book of the Dead* to successfully pass this judgement – including memorising the forty-two chimeric gods and demons that one will encounter on one's journey, as well as the itinerary of halls that one passes through. The deceased must confirm they have not contravened any of the possible forty-two crimes that would bar entry – 'I have not reviled the God; I have not laid violent hands on an orphan; I have not done what the God abominates… I have not killed; I have not turned anyone over to a killer… I have not taken milk from a child's mouth; I have not driven small cattle from their herbage…' and so on, until the full confession is made. Anubis then performs

ABOVE: *One of the coffins of Gua, physician to the governor Djehutyhotep, dated to 1795 BC. The painted floor shows the 'two ways' of land and sea that the dead could take to reach the afterlife. The twisting lines form a map of the underworld to help the deceased reach the afterlife. A false door was also included, to allow the* ka *(spirit) of the dead to escape.*

his judgement, weighing the heart of the deceased against a feather, which symbolises the Egyptian concept of justice, harmony and balance known as *ma'at*. A righteous heart is as light as air. Any heart found to be heavier than the feather was rejected, and devoured by Ammit, the eater of souls – these unfortunates simply ceased to exist. The souls that passed the test are permitted to travel onward, to A'aru.

Even if one follows every instruction offered in the *Book of the Dead*, and other similar texts, it is still not an easy journey to the Other World. The wandering dead have to negotiate both hostile terrain and spiritual booby traps. The tortures and punishments that fill this network of chambers, halls and shadowy corners are physical and often bloody; but most curious is the inverse gravity of the realm.

Just as the Fields of Rushes is a paradise of exaggerated earthly perfection, so the Egyptian netherworld is a mirror image of natural order – the sinners, now in the underworld beneath the flat disc of Earth, must surely walk upside down as they tread the underside of the living world, otherwise they would simply fall off. This, it was believed, forced one's digestion to be reversed, meaning excrement would cascade from one's mouth. In utterance 210 of the Pyramid Texts, the oldest Egyptian set of funerary and magical texts, we find reference to a pharaoh crossing into the afterlife and demanding a meal of roasted calf, then exhibiting anxiety that this could lead to disastrous results when combined with walking upside down: 'What I detest is faeces, I reject urine... I will never eat the detestableness of these two.'

There is a lake of raging fire to avoid (a common feature of so many hellscapes), which is used like a giant barbecue cooker by hungry demons lying in wait. The wandering deceased should also avoid the underworld baboons – considered a mystical animal by the Egyptians – which are fond of decapitating unwary visitors. Beware too the ravenous hell-swine, crocodiles, serpents and wild dogs that also haunt the dark plains. 'We find in all books about the Other World,' wrote the Egyptologist E. A. Wallis Budge, 'pits of fire, abysses of darkness, deadly knives, rivers of boiling water, fetid exhalations, fire-breathing dragons, frightful monsters,

and creatures with the heads of animals, cruel and murderous creatures of various aspect… similar to those from early medieval literature. It is almost certain that modern nations owe much of their concept of hell to Egypt.'

ABOVE: *An illustration from the* Book of the Dead *of Hunefer, a scribe of the Nineteenth Dynasty (fl. c.1300 BC). From left to right, Anubis leads Hunefer by the hand to be judged, and performs the act with the scales. Hunefer's heart, shown in a pot, is weighed against a feather. Hunefer passes, and is led to Osiris by his son Horus. Had he failed, he would have been consumed by Ammit in the centre, the ferocious 'devourer', part-crocodile, part-lion, part-hippopotamus.*

LEFT: *A detail of the Pyramid Texts, from the pyramid of the pharaoh Teti (reigned 2323-2291 BC) in Saqqara, the necropolis of the ancient Egyptian capital Memphis.*

OPPOSITE: *A* ushabti *(funerary figurine) depicting Ramesses IV, made sometime between 1143 and 1136 BC during the Twentieth Dynasty of Egypt (1189-1077 BC).*

THE KUR NETHERWORLD OF
ANCIENT MESOPOTAMIA

Ancient Mesopotamians were born to die. In the Old Babylonian *Atrahasis* epic, the gods are said to have created humans by mixing clay with the blood of the rebellious god We-ilu, who was slaughtered especially for the procedure. Humans are therefore composed of both earthly and divine ingredients, but the divine element does not ensure immortality. Enki, the Sumerian god of wisdom and magic, declared that death awaited man from his first moments – indeed the most frequent euphemism for dying in Mesopotamian texts is 'to go to one's fate'. The *Epic of Gilgamesh* ultimately persuades its reader that the quest for immortality was pointless. Instead, one should live on in the fame of one's accomplishments on Earth. The only immortal life is in the memories of others.[1]

Unlike the abundance of Egyptian funerary texts, no such afterlife instruction manuals of the ancient Mesopotamians have been discovered. Instead, to gain insights into the

---

1 Which recalls Woody Allen's thoughts on the same issue: 'I don't want to achieve immortality through my work; I want to achieve immortality through not dying. I don't want to live on in the hearts of my countrymen; I want to live on in my apartment.'

imaginations of these Near Eastern cultures, we must assemble pieces from the wealth of literature across different genres that was generated between the third and the first millennia BC, in which death and hell are often discussed.

The heavens were home to the gods alone – the dead travelled instead to a dark, colourless netherworld known by many names: in Sumerian it is called Kur, Irkalla, Kukku, Arali or Kigal; in Akkadian it is Erṣetu. Metaphysically, Kur is far away; physically, it was thought to lie in a cavern a short distance below the world's surface. It is referred to as the 'land of no return', and the 'house which none leaves who enters', and is imagined as a giant house of dust. Dust cakes its doors, its buildings and bolts, and indeed dust is the only food and drink available to the dead. (Above ground, grieving families would traditionally pour out liquids onto the dirt for their deceased to enjoy.)

It was thought one could find a gateway to Kur somewhere in the Zagros mountains, to the far east, where a staircase sloped down to the gates of the underworld. Or, according to other traditions, the entrance lay at an impossibly remote point somewhere in the far west (hinted at by the fact that real rivers known to exist far from Sumer were sometimes referred to as 'rivers of the underworld'). Kur itself lay directly beneath another subterranean mythical feature, the Abzu, a body of freshwater beneath the earth.

In further contrast to ancient Egypt, the dead mingle with no trace of social hierarchy. There are descriptions of Kur being an unbreakable fortress city (known as the *iri-gal* in Sumerian), having seven barred gates through which return to the living was impossible. Existence in this netherworld is a shadowy, anaemic version of life above; though the darkness is routinely pierced by Shamash, the sun god of justice, who travels through the underworld every night during his journey through the cosmos. The underworld is neither a place of joy nor abject misery, merely a dried and dulled version of life above ground – not a hell, as we understand the word, but an antipode to the vibrant high heavens. And, unusually, there is no system of judgement, no

reward or punishment based on one's actions. Instead, it is the conditions of burial that establish the conditions of your next existence.

The most vivid descriptions of the underworld come from the Sumerian tale *Descent of Inanna into the Underworld*, in which the goddess of sexual love and war, and enforcer of divine justice known as the 'Queen of Heaven' (originally worshipped as 'Ishtar' in Akkadia), travels through Kur. The underworld is ruled by her sister, the goddess Ereshkigal, who lives in the underground palace Ganzir, and is married – depending on the version of the story – to either Gugalanna, a 'canal-inspector of Anu', or, in later stories, the more exciting Nergal, god of death.

In the Sumerian version of the story, Inanna travels to the gates of the underworld, demanding entry. Ereshkigal allows each of the seven gates through which she must pass to be opened by just a crack, forcing Inanna to squeeze through by removing a piece of clothing at each gate, gradually stripping her of her power. By the time Inanna reaches Ereshkigal's court she is naked, but still manages to take Ereshkigal's place. The group of deities in residence known as the Anunnaki are outraged by this, and turn Inanna into a corpse hanging by a hook.

Ereshkigal eventually consents to her sister's corpse being sprinkled with the food and water of life to be revived, but there's a catch – Ereshkigal demands one of the living take her place. Not her servant Ninshubur, Inanna says, for he is loyal; not Shara, her beautician, for he is seen mourning her death. Ereshkigal's *galla* (demons) then propose taking Dumuzid, Inanna's shepherd consort. He is revealed to be dealing with his grief rather admirably, spending his days lavishly clothed, sitting on his wife's throne while being entertained by slave girls. An irate Inanna immediately instructs the demons to take him, and Dumuzid is dragged down to the netherworld, lipstick marks still fresh on his collar, while Inanna is allowed to return to the upper world.

ZOROASTRIAN AFTERWORLDS: THE HOUSE OF LIES AND THE HOUSE OF SONG

LEFT: *The Tomb of Wirkak, commonly referred to as the Tomb of Master Shi, was fashioned around AD 580 (Northern Zhou dynasty) but discovered only in 2003, in the Weiyang District, Xi'an, China. The sarcophagus is richly engraved with bas-reliefs of Zoroastrian divinities and scenes of sacrifice, and on the east wall Master Shi and his wife are crossing the Chinvat bridge to be received into paradise.*

One of the world's oldest continually observed religions is Zoroastrianism (or Mazdayasna as it is also known), which is based on the teachings of the Iranian prophet Zarathustra ('Zartosht' in Persian, 'Zoroaster' in Greek) who lived sometime between 1500 and 1000 BC. In this ancient belief system, we find core tenets that would underpin later global religions. Zarathustra rejected the gods of the ancient Irano-Aryan religion, instead preaching that there was only one god to worship: Ahura Mazda, the Lord of Wisdom and creator of the world. In so doing, the prophet not only widened the gulf between Iranian and Indian-Aryan belief, but also introduced quite probably the first monotheistic religion in history.

For more than a thousand years of Iranian imperial history – from Achaemenid (550-330 BC), through the Parthian Empire (247 BC-AD 224), to the crumbling of the Zoroastrian state at the end of the Sasanian period (AD 224-651), Zoroastrianism was a religion of significant cultural impact in the Near and Middle East. Under its influence, for example, Judaism gradually developed eschatological concepts of death, judgement, final destinations of the soul and evil, tributaries of thinking that fed into Christianity and later Islam.

One god did not of course preclude the existence of many subsets of supernatural creatures and psychopomps (spiritual soul guides), and indeed these are well introduced with a look at the path along which the deceased Zoroastrian faithful trudged to hell: the Chinvat bridge. At the heart of the *Avesta*, the compendium of Zoroastrianism texts, is its liturgy, the *Yasna*, which includes seventeen hymns composed by Zarathustra himself called the *Gathas*.

Here among these ancient poetical verses we find the earliest key afterworld references and descriptions, like that in *Yasna* 46:11, where it's mentioned that the soul and the *daēnā* (a term that has multiple translations, but is essentially one's character) of the wicked arrive at the Chinvat bridge, to be guests in the House of Lies. According to eschatological tradition, the Chinvat bridge – 'bridge of the separator' or, according to more recent thought, 'bridge of the collector' –

OPPOSITE: *A spectacular parchment painting of the Zoroastrian hell and paradise from the sixteenth century, with an unusual diagonal division. On the left, souls are devoured and tortured by demons, snakes and scorpions; on the right, others are welcomed into the light of the Sun.*

is a nexus between this world and the next that all departing souls must cross, similar to the later concept of the As-Sirāt in Islam (see page 60). Its earthly bridgehead lies at the summit of the mythical mountain Harburz, while its end in the south leads to the paradise of the House of Song. Its vast body is suspended directly above hell, 'high' and 'fearful' according to the Middle Persian text *Mēnōg-ī Khrad*. A collection of texts within the *Avesta* called the *Vidēvdād* reports that two fearsome dogs guard the bridge; and in a collection called the *Bundahišn* the bridge is said to resemble a sharp sword – another source calls it 'a razor blade of many sides'.

This last descriptor refers to the spectacular 'sifting' function of the Chinvat bridge. Three days after death, the soul makes it way towards the entrance of the bridge, in the guiding company of both benevolent gods and a gang of threatening demons, until the raucous party meets an awaiting tribunal presided over by the judicial figure of Mithra, the Zoroastrian Angelic Divinity of Covenant, Light and Oath, protector of Truth and guardian of cattle. The good and evil deeds of the soul are added up on a spiritual balance, and if the deceased is deemed virtuous their *dēn* appears in the form of a beautiful maiden, a personification of their purity, to lead the soul across the Chinvat bridge, which has expanded to a width of thirty-seven *nāy* (poles) wide, according to the *Dādestān ī dēnīg*. The crossing to paradise is an easy one, made 'well-wishingly and free from sorrow' on a luxurious carpet of stoat skins in glorious, fragrant spring weather.

For those whose balance of good and bad is a dead tie, the destination is Hamistagan (see page 132), a limbo-like realm where, according to the *Dādestān ī dēnīg*, the dead can relive their lives, improving their conduct in a bid to earn entry into the House of Song. If the deceased is judged to be wicked, however, their *dēn* takes the form of a wizened, grotesque hag, who takes the soul on a disgusting crossing of the Chinvat bridge similar to entering a charnel house (a vault of rotting human remains). The bridge contracts to the width and sharpness of a razor blade, from which the *druuant* (unrighteous dead) tumble, dragged down by demons into the hell of the House of Lies.

Condemnation to this hell is not, however, an eternal sentence – its nature is more forgiving and temporary than others examined in this book; the realm is intended to be more reformative, with punishments tailored to the crimes perpetrated. It is of course still far from being a pleasant place: noxious fumes choke the air and the darkness is overwhelming. (In fact, in the Zoroastrian cosmological text *Bundahišn* (27:53), the darkness of hell is said to be so thick that it can be held in one's hand, and the odours so powerful that they can be cut with a knife.) Poisonous foods are all that can be found, and even though souls are crammed together in wailing droves, they are still filled with the chill of abject loneliness.

A graphic tour of hell is provided by the author of the *Book of Ardā Wīrāz*, an account of a dream journey that is thought to have been composed sometime during the period of the Sasanian Empire (224-651). Having been shown paradise by Ahura Mazda, Ardā Wīrāz is then led on a journey through hell to glimpse the punishments inflicted on the damned, and at one point he spots Alexander the Great, who for his conquests of Persia has been condemned to the hell described as a deep well – dark, stinking and claustrophobically narrow. *Xrafstars* (hell creatures) are reported to be as tall as mountains, feasting on the souls of the damned. The specific punishments that await those who violate Zoroastrian law, particularly for sexual crimes, are examined in depth across eighty chapters (some of which are shown here).

In the *Dādestān ī dēnīg* (Chapter 26), the ninth-century high priest Manuščihr reveals that there is hope for those suffering in hell. The condemned souls will one day endure the ordeal of wading through rivers of molten metal for three days – the righteous will emerge unscathed and the impure will be cleansed of their transgressions, as part of the final episode of Zoroastrian eschatology. This is a time in the future when the moon falls dark, the world descends into winter and Ahriman makes his escape from hell to terrorise the Earth. When all seems at a loss, rescue will come in the form of the saviour Saošyant, born to a virgin who fell pregnant by the seed of Zarathustra while swimming in a lake. Saošyant will resurrect all the dead in heaven, hell (who are gathered in a giant net by the divinity Airyaman) and the limbo plain of Hamistagan, and induct them in the cleansing ordeal of molten metal.

Thus, while hell is real, it is not forever: evil will be vanquished (but not destroyed), mountains will crumble, valleys will rise, the Earth and the House of Song will converge on the Moon, and mankind will gain immortality.

ABOVE AND OPPOSITE: *The unbearable hellish tortures that await violators of Zoroastrian law, according to the ancient Persian prophet Zarathustra and described in the* Book of Ardā Wīrāz, *this copy thought to date from the year 1589.*

THE HELLS OF ANCIENT INDIA

Exploring the numerous Indian religious sects that fall under the vast umbrella term of Hinduism is to encounter an ancient melee of disparate doctrines, philosophies, traditions and gods. Fortunately, for our purpose, there are infernal commonalities, even if this might seem to clash with the common understanding of the Hindu eschatological outlook – namely that, as with Buddhism and Jainism, it is an ideology centred on the concept of *samsāra*. The soul is eternal, caught in a perpetual cycle of transmigration and reincarnation. Despite this, heavens and hells exist in Hindu tradition, as realms of rewards and retribution for the good and evil actions one commits in life, although ultimately these are not the *final* destinations for the freshly deceased, merely a form of judicial balance to keep behaviour in check before one begins the wheel of life anew. As way stations on the grand journey, Hindu heavens and hells are less important than in other religions, yet much consideration has been lavished on their detail.

As ever, it is by scouring the original sacred texts that we can tune into the necrovision of the ancients, and understand how this image developed with time. One finds that, in fact, the notion of *samsāra* did not exist in the earliest of the religions; but references to hell *can* be found in the three categories of ancient Hindu literature. The oldest texts are known as the *Vedas*, the *Itihasa* (also referred to as 'epic literature') and the *Puranas* (literally 'ancient'). The *Vedas* are the most authoritative, and while thought to have first been written down in Sanskrit perhaps in the second century BC they are considerably older, having been passed down through a long history of oral tradition since the second millennium BC.

The earliest is the *Rigveda* (the Veda of Adoration), which provides the first glimpse of the hell of the damned, deep beneath the world's rivers. In Hymn 39 of Book 2, the author begs of Indra not to be sent to hell, where 'sin round the wicked boils like as a cauldron set amid the flames of fire…' There are 'endless caverns', where one can find 'press-stones with loud ring [to] destroy the demons' and to 'save us from the pit and falling'. It is a realm where the damned (the fool, the traitor, the thief, the glutton, etc.) are boiled and burnt,

skewered and dismantled. In the *Atharvaveda* (Veda of the Old and Wise) it's mentioned that those who spit on and sin against a Brahman (a member of the highest Hindu caste), or fail to give him the cow he asks for, will end up in hell sitting in a river of blood, 'devouring hair', drinking the water with which previously 'men wash the corpse and wet the beard'.

Narasimha, the man-lion avatar of Vishnu. In this form, Vishnu disembowels with his claws the demon king Hiraṇ yakaśipu, who had arrogantly forbidden the worship of Vishnu throughout his kingdom.

In Book 18, Chapter 2 of the first of the two major Sanskrit works that comprise the Epic Literature, the *Mahabharata*, there is the story of King Yudhishthira, who travels to hell to argue against the suffering of friends and family members, the first in a hell-tour motif that far predates the Christian 'harrowing of hell' tradition in which Jesus travels to the infernal realm:

Polluted with the stench of sinners, and miry with flesh and blood, it abounded with gadflies and stinging bees and gnats and was endangered by the inroads of wild bears. Rotting corpses lay here and there. Overspread with bones and hair, it was noisome with worms and insects. It was skirted all along with a blazing fire. It was infested by crows and other birds and vultures, all having beaks of iron, as also by evil spirits with long mouths pointed like needles...

The righteous-souled king proceeded, filled with diverse thoughts. He beheld a river full of boiling water and therefore difficult to cross, as also a forest of trees whose leaves were sharp swords and razors. There were plains full of fine white sand exceedingly heated, and rocks and stones made of iron. There were many jars of iron all around, with boiling oil in them...

Translation by Kisari Mohan Ganguli, 1883-1896

In the other epic, the *Ramayana*, a visit to hell is made by Ravana, the demon king of the island fortress Lanka, who reaches the hell-city of Yama, god of death, and his demonic forces, in the hell known as Naraka. This he achieves by successfully crossing the blood-filled – or nectar-filled if one is righteous – Vaitarani River, which divides hell from the living world. The righteous need not cross the waterway but sinners must, though they can be aided by a vessel if they have committed at least some personal sacrifice, such as donating money or a cow. If not, they must wait years for a servant of Yama to come and drag them across.

So where exactly can we locate the Hindu hell? For this we can look to the *Puranas*, the vast, encyclopedic works of ancient and medieval Indian cosmological history and legend, together totalling over 400,000 narrative verses thought to have first been composed between *c*.300 and 1500. While their contents range across a universe of subject matter, only a few contain descriptions of hell. The *Bhagavata Purana* locates hell under the earth between the seven-layered underworld known as Patala (a place separate to an underground hell in Hindu tradition, being unusually a subterranean paradise more beautiful than even the heaven known as Svarga, and the Garbhodaka Ocean, believed to be at the bottom of the universe). The *Devi Bhagavata Purana* also mentions hell being at the southernmost point of the cosmos; as does the *Vishnu Purana*, below the cosmic waters.

In the *Markandeya Purana*, the 'dolorous' regions burn in deep darkness, revealing 'sights that even the boldest of human beings could not behold without shuddering, horror, pale and eyes aghast'. There, iron-beaked birds were tearing out flesh from the bodies of the sinful, while fierce-looking ministers of death were constantly belabouring them with stout iron clubs and deluging the place with their blood. This was the ordinary mode of punishment, but there were other punishments besides. The latter includes being left to writhe in agony while buried in a 'gigantic jar, full of burning hot sand'.

In the *Puranas*, hell becomes segmented, and details of its various regions are developed. The *Vamana Purana* has been dated to *c*.450-900, and is notable for providing the first list of various departments of Hindu hell, which are usually said to number twenty-one but in fact twenty-five are named in the original text (and indeed the number varies more with other texts). What is most emphasised is the enormous size of these regions – Raurava is a 2000-league-wide field of hot glowing coals; twice as large, at 4000 leagues, is Maharaurava (a boiling swamp of molten copper that is the destination for those who set fire to fields, barns and villages); Taamistra, where thieves are beaten with weapons, is twice this at 8000 leagues; Andhataamistra is 16,000 leagues; and so on. People who steal sandals will be sent to the hell named Kalmsikta; disobedient children go to Aprathisth. People who touch their elders with their bare feet go to Raurava. The person who selfishly nourishes just himself during a drought will end up in the hell known as Swabhojan. People who copulate on holy days will find themselves in Shaalmali, the hell of burning thorns.

In the *Padma Purana*, Yama, Lord of Death, is described as resembling 'a heap of black clay, who is fierce, ruthless, fearful and surrounded by fearful messengers, who is full of all diseases… who is mounted on a buffalo, who is extremely fierce and fearful because of his large teeth. His face resembles death. The wicked-minded man sees Yama, who has adorned

A c.1780 painting of Matsya, the fish avatar of Vishnu, defeating the demon Śankhāsura.

himself with red flowers, and whose body is huge. Yama…
punishes him with tortures and with wooden mallets.' The *Padma Purana* also offers a separate breakdown of hell's structure, listing seven principal regions (each with six divisions, and each of those with divisions for deliberate and non-deliberate sins, bringing the total to eighty-four); but it is in the elaboration of the punishments that the author, or authors, relish with detail:

Sometimes the sinful ones are roasted in a fire of dry cow-dung; sometimes they are eaten up by fierce lions, wolves, tigers, gadflies and worms. Sometimes they are eaten by great leeches or by huge cobras and by terrible flies or sometimes by extremely poisonous serpents. Sometimes they are eaten by crazed and vicious herds of elephants or by great bulls with sharp horns scratching the path, and by buffaloes with big horns gouging the bodies of the wicked, and by fierce female goblins and by terrible demons. Mounted on

*The Court of Yama,
Lord of Death, c.1800.*

a great balance and tormented by very terrible diseases and burnt in a wild fire, they go to Yama. They are very violently shaken by terrible winds and shattered completely by showers of great slabs of stone and by terrifying falling meteors that sound like thunderbolts. Once struck by the shower of burning charcoal they go to Yama.

Punishments in hell as per Jain cosmology, painted in the seventeenth century.

Ultimately – and broadly speaking of course – at the core of the Hindu approach to the afterlife is the knowledge that life in this world is not something that one can enhance in the next cycle of reincarnation. Salvation instead is in the concept of *moksha* (shared with Jainism and Buddhism), a relinquishment of the self so one is absorbed into the divine Brahman, the impersonal Absolute, of which one's being is merely an element. The *Chandogya Upanishad* relates how the

Brahman is the 'self within the heart' of man while also being the entire cosmos, smaller than a grain of rice yet greater than the world and sky. By merging, one finds the only immortality, and the serenity of entering a state in which one cannot be said either to exist or not to exist. Not one soul will be denied this ultimate fate.

The seven hells of Jain cosmology, from a 1613 painting from a Jain temple in Gujarat.

HELLS OF THE EAST

Having emerged from the Ganges culture of northern India around 500 BC, Buddhism shares much with Hinduism; but certain Hindu tenets were jettisoned in the fifth- to fourth-century teachings of Siddhārtha Gautama, the mendicant philosopher born of aristocratic stock who would – two centuries after his death – be given the title Buddha ('Awakened One', or 'Enlightened One'). Gone were the gods, priests and the formal rituals including animal sacrifice. Also rejected was the hierarchy of the caste system. Instead, Buddha encouraged the seeking of enlightenment through meditation, to reach the final goal of nirvana ('extinguishment'), when one enters into union with the universe and escapes the cycle of death and rebirth. In Buddhism the self is an illusion, and the desire to obtain personal immortality actually an obstacle in achieving nirvana, an experience that is impossible to describe for it is so far from human understanding. While Buddhism in India was eventually absorbed by Hinduism, and Buddha himself was assimilated into the pantheon of Hindu deities, Buddha's teachings lived on, spread through central, east and southern Asia.

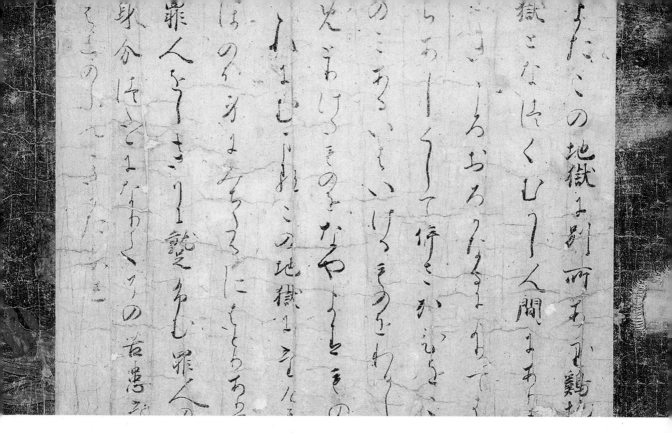

One Hindu feature preserved in Buddhism is the variety of Naraka hell-realms, which must be viewed in the same manner as in that ancient religion – hells not as the ultimate destination for condemned souls, but as temporary retributive punishment for the impious, while caught in the revolving wheel of existence and rebirth. This is not to say that the length of time (which functions as it does on Earth) spent in hell is unchallenging – far from it. Buddhist texts mention unfathomably long sentences, from hundreds of millions to sextillions (10^{21}) of years. The *Sutra on the Eighteen Hells* (AD 100-200), for example, relates that in the *Hsien-chiu-hu* layer of hell the inhabitants fistfight with each other for 135 billion years; in *Chü-lu-ts'ui-lüeh*, the dead are tortured with fire for 270 billion years; and, in *Tu-i-nan-ch'ieh*, one spends 8,640 billion years enduring torments that switch between scorching by fire, and lying in a pit of ravenous worms.

Just how many hells there are, though, varies between the surviving texts. With the teachings having spread so widely, with centuries of local religious influences, the afterworld explorer is presented with a daunting itinerary, for a count of Buddhist hells can range from eight to several thousand. These number so highly because many texts describe segmented hell departments specifically designed to match the sin committed.

The Hell of the Flaming Rooster, the eleventh of sixteen identified hells, presided over by a giant fire-breathing fowl. From the twelfth-century Japanese Buddhist mythology manuscript known as The Hell Scroll, *which also describes the Hell of Excrement, the Hell of the Iron Mortar, the Hell of the Black Sand Cloud, the Hell of Pus and Blood, and the Hell of Foxes and Wolves.*

Traditionally however (i.e. from the revelations of the earliest sources), the principal Buddhist hells most commonly number eight. Picture enormous caverns layered above each other, with each holding sixteen minor infernal departments – each of the four gates in each major hell gives access to four of the minor hells. Time is also an aggravating factor – each sentence in these Narakas lasts eight times longer than the one before it. Listed, this hell core-sample comprises the following strata:

Samjiva *the hell of constant repetition. Here the ground is hot iron, heated by a giant fire beneath. The moment one worries about being attacked, figures appear to do just that, attacking with iron claws and flaming weapons. When finally beaten unconscious one is magically revived, and the beatings start anew. This hell is said to be 1,000 yojanas (a unit of measurement equal to about 7-9 miles / 12-15km) beneath Jambudvīpa (one of the seven concentric island continents of the world in Puranic cosmography) and stretching for 10,000 yojanas in each direction.*

Kalasutra *the hell of black wire or thread. Black lines are drawn on the sufferer's body by the guards of hell, who use them as guidelines for their gleeful sawing and chopping with axes.*

Samghata *the hell of crushing with stone slabs. Here, enormous boulders pound the bodies of the sinful into a fine red paste. Then, the rocks return to their place, the bodies are restored and the torture begins again.*

Raurava *the hell of lamentation. In this realm, souls and creatures run about in perpetual screaming panic, searching for shelter from the fiery ground. When they think they have finally found a safe place to hide, they find themselves locked inside and renew their screaming as the fires burn around them.*

Maharaurava *the hell of great lamentation, where even greater suffering is provided by animals known as kravyada, which tear at flesh.*

Tapana *the hell of scorching heat, where residents are impaled on the flaming spears of the hell guards, finding the flames bursting from their eyes and mouths.*

Pratapana *the hell of fiercely scorching heat, where the tortures are much the same as those of Tapana, except the impaling is done more brutally and bodily with tridents, and lasts for an antarakalpa – an exceptionally long time.*

OPPOSITE: *Yama, Lord of Death, gripping the Bhavacakra, the Wheel of Life, an illustration of the Buddhist cycle of life, death and rebirth. The snake, pig and rooster in the central circle represent craving, hatred and ignorance. The sections surrounding them represent the six realms of the gods, the titans, the humans, the animals, the hungry ghosts and the demons.*

ཁ་ལྲགས་མི་ཟན་གར་པར་གོན་པ

Avici *lasting equally as long is the imprisonment in this realm, the hell without interruption. This lowest level of hell hosts the greatest suffering, where one finds residents being cooked in giant ovens without respite, reserved for the most serious sinners. It is described as cube-shaped, of about 20,000 yojanas (about 186,410 miles / 300,000km) in each measurement.*

A Buddhist tsagli *(also* tsakali; *initiation card) warning of a realm of hell in which monks who don't keep up with their studies will be repeatedly crushed under enormous books.*

If we incorporate Tibetan Buddhist tradition, then located above these main hot hells, and just below the surface of the earth, lie a further eight principal cold hells, named for the upsetting ways in which the body reacts to frozen conditions, such as the hell of chattering teeth and the hell of blue-lotus-coloured patches on the skin. Each one of these also has sixteen minor hells, bringing the total to a minimum of 256.

As Buddhism spread from India through East Asia, the belief features of the ancient ideas were expanded and built on, incorporating elements of local mythological storytelling. Take as an example the 'sword-blade trees' mentioned in the *Ōjōyōshū* (The Essentials of Rebirth in the Pure Land), an important Buddhist text written in 985 by the Japanese monk Genshin, which portrays a forest of unusual trees that exists to excruciate those sinfully lustful:

As they look up to the top branches of the trees in the forest they see beautiful and well-dressed women, indeed the faces of those whom once they loved. This fills them with joy and so they try to climb up the trees, but when they do so the branches and leaves all turn into swords, which lacerate the flesh and pierce the bones. When they reach the top they find the object of their desire below on the ground luring them to come down… But as they descend, the leaves of the trees, which are made of swords, turn upwards and thus lacerate their bodies. When they are about to reach the ground, the women appear on the tops of the trees… This process goes on for ten trillion years.

Many details of Buddhist hell come from the sutras, the texts that form the core of canonical literature of Buddhism, as they are considered to be, in part, documentation of the Buddha's oral sermons. In the *Mahavastu* (Sanskrit for 'The Great Story'), compiled sometime between the second century BC and fourth century AD, hell is described as being composed of eight great hells with sixteen hells each, or 128 hells in total. The hells are pictured as cubed fortresses 100 *yojanas* square and high, arranged in a grid (with gates to the lesser hells in each corner)

At the Dong Yue Miao temple, Beijing, visitors can see these recreations of the punishments meted out by officers of the various hell departments. Here, a liar prepares to have his tongue cut out.

and surrounded by a great iron barrier, with a sealed iron ceiling above and a ground of hot iron beneath.

From the *Majjhima Nikaya* (The Middle-Length Discourses of the Buddha) of *c*.200-100 BC, we learn that flames pour from the walls, floor and ceiling of these fortresses and there are exit doors in each wall that swing open, only to slam shut as soon as you near them. When eventually you make it through the eastern door, you find yourself in the Hell of Excrement, where you are devoured by creatures. All you can do is flee to the Hell of Hot Embers, and then to the aforementioned Wood of Sword-blade Trees, where your extremities are severed, before tumbling into the River of Caustic Water. When you crawl to shore, hell officiants pour liquid copper and hot metal balls down your throat. Until your original sin is compensated for, you will not die to be reborn outside this torment.

Though the spellings and minor details of these hells vary in Indian, Tibetan, Japanese and most other Buddhist texts, for the most part these features are consistent. In Chinese hell texts, however, Buddhist concepts were often developed under the influence of Taoism and other local folk religions' influence, which result in certain permutations and the presence in Chinese mythology of the purgatorial hell realm known as Diyu. The most noticeable new municipal development is the notion of a ten-court hell, as illustrated by physical recreations that can be found around the country, like the necropolis in Fengdu and the Dong Yue Miao temple in Beijing (see image on previous page). In the First Court, the sinner enters their first process of judgement on their actions, having stood on the Tower of Reflection to look back at their time on Earth; in Courts Two to Nine, they must endure purgatorial torments; and, on reaching the Tenth, they are assigned their new life, with the aid of a Wheel of Transformation and also the Terrace of Oblivion, where the sinner's memories are wiped.

According to legend, the Jade Emperor appointed Yama (also known as Yanluo Wang) to oversee the daily running of Diyu, which possesses up to 12,800 segmented hell departments, in its location at the brim of the cosmos. The first hell figures you are likely to encounter on arrival, however, are 'Ox-Head' and 'Horse-Face', or 'Gozu' and 'Mezu' in Japan, two guardian spirits of the underworld. All deceased are sent to Diyu on death, but those who have a relatively clean slate of misdeeds escape relatively quickly, while the rest are processed through

Traditional depictions of the tortures of Diyu, the Chinese hell influenced by the Hindu and Buddhist concept of Naraka. From top to bottom: the Chamber of Rocks, the Chamber of Oxen and the Chamber of Tongue-ripping.

Yama's ten courts, each presided over by a Yama king. Diyu even has a capital city, Youdu (similar to Pandemonium in Milton's *Paradise Lost*), which is said to be similar to earthly Chinese capital cities, dotted with demonic palaces and offices, except that it is composed of dense darkness.

In Chinese culture, hells are more bureaucratic. The dead are forced to while time away in waiting rooms, negotiating their way through a labyrinth of offices to find the official in charge of assigning their destination, repeatedly submitting petitions

From the eighteenth century, these Thai folding manuscripts were commissioned by relatives of the recently deceased to earn merit for their loved ones in the afterlife. The more money spent on the book, the higher the rate of spiritual return. As shown here, they commonly tell the story of Phra Malai, a legendary Buddhist monk who flew to hell.

following strict procedures to the letter before they can make progress. This being hell, there are of course administrative mix-ups to deal with. In the Chinese tale *Mulian Saves His Mother from Hell* (before AD 921), the protagonist finds that the insatiable occupants of the Hungry Ghost realm have wound up there by bureaucratic error, victims of mistaken identity too late to correct now that earthbound family members have performed funeral rites. Though, in this case, hell remains a realm of traditionally bodily tortures, as one commonly finds, the nature of hell evolves with the times. It is most interesting that, in this case, the true fascination that grips the popular imagination is with the torture provided by the endlessly repetitive 'small cuts' of mindless municipal bureaucracy – as anyone who has ever become entangled with local government can attest.

ABOVE: *Hell money, resembling legal tender, traditionally burnt as offerings in Chinese ancestral worship to help ease financial issues in the afterlife. Some bear portraits of the Jade Emperor, the first god in traditional Chinese religions, while modern examples can feature glamorous celebrities, like this example from the 1960s showing John F. Kennedy.*

LEFT: *Naraka (Buddhist hell) in Burmese representation from* The Thirty-Seven Nats, A Phase of Spirit-Worship Prevailing in Burma *(1906) by Sir Richard Carnac Temple.*

OPPOSITE: *A Thai manuscript illustration of the dead being punished by hell officials.*

HADES

'Do not make light to me, O shining Odysseus,' cries Achilles
to Odysseus in Homer's *Odyssey*, Book XI. 'I would rather be
a menial on earth, bound to an impoverished master, than to
be a great king among these dead men who have had their day.'
The earliest recorded idea of the Greek afterlife is provided
by Homer, who paints images of the dead as wandering
shadows, ghosts of their former selves lacking any strength
or agency. The name given for this nebulous netherworld
was Hades, as is the name given to the god who presided over
the sunless place and who snatched spirits to populate it.

Geographically, Hades shifts and evolves over time. In the
Iliad, Homer describes the giant river Oceanus, which encircled
the flat, disc-shaped Earth, functioning as the source of all
Earth's fresh water. The Sun, Moon and stars all rose from,
and set in, its waters. Hades was said to be beyond Oceanus,
even farther to the west; this changed to the belief that it was
an underworld, and other writers claimed it to be accessible

Aeneas and the Sibyl in the
Underworld *(c.1630) by Jan
Brueghel the Younger, inspired
by the work of Jan Brueghel the
Elder, who in turn followed
the work of Hieronymus Bosch.*

to the living via hidden portals in the surrounding natural geography of valleys and mountains.

There is, for example, the cave that exists to this day on Cape Matapan (known in antiquity as Cape Taenarum) on the Mani Peninsula of Greece, which was said to be the cave from which Hercules dragged Cerberus and through which Orpheus entered the underworld to retrieve Eurydice.

The bottomless Alcyonian Lake (now marshland) at Lerna, near the east coast of the Peloponnesus, south of Argos, was a hell portal guarded by the monstrous Hydra, and supposedly the entrance used by Dionysus to enter the netherworld to find his mother Semele. 'There is no limit to the depth of the Alcyonian Lake,' writes Pausanias in *Description of Greece*, 'and I know of nobody who by any contrivance has been able to reach the bottom of it since not even Nero, who had ropes made several stades long and fastened them together, tying lead to them, and omitting nothing that might help his experiment, was able to discover any limit to its depth… every swimmer who ventures to cross it is dragged down, sucked into the depths, and swept away.' One also has the access option of the volcanic crater

The Sibyl showing Aeneas the Underworld with Charon's Boat (c.1620) by Jacob Van Swanenburg. The underworld of Classical antiquity, with Pluto, god of the underworld, driving his chariot through the air, Charon and his boat in the lower left, and the Seven Sins portrayed in the giant hell-mouth in the lower right.

Lake Avernus, in the Campania region of southern Italy, which was also thought by the Romans to be the entrance to the underworld. It is the portal that Aeneas takes as he makes his descent in Virgil's *Aeneid*.

Having descended, there was, however, one great obstacle to reach the perimeter of Hades – one of the most famous of all necro-geographic features. The terrible river Styx encircled the underworld seven times, and was known as the river of hatred and unbreakable oaths, for the gods are occasionally mentioned as making vows by its waters. The river was only crossable with the aid of the boatman Charon.[1]

Other rivers beside the Styx are reported as running through the underworld: the Acheron is the dark and depthless river of sorrow and pain; the Cocytus is the river of wailing laments; the Phlegethon is the river of fire, perhaps leading to the depths of Tartarus. Finally there is the Lethe, the river whose waters when sipped cause memory loss, and from which the dead drink to forget their previous lives in the hope of reincarnation.

For the intrepid explorer of Hades, there are different regions to investigate: Tartarus is reserved for the worst transgressors; the Elysian Fields (explored further on page 168) is the paradise destination for only the most virtuous; the *Lugentes Campi* (Fields of Mourning) were home to those who wasted away their lives on unrequited love; and the Asphodel Meadows are for average or indifferent souls who never committed any serious crimes, but who also are not remarkable enough for admittance to the Elysian Fields.

Having crossed the Styx, one encounters a wild array of beasts patrolling the area before the main doors, including centaurs, Scylla, Briareus, the Gorgons, the Lernaean Hydra, Geryon, the Chimera and harpies. And then there is the most notorious of all, Kerberos (Cerberus in Latin), the ferocious, many-headed hellhound guarding the entrance. Should you successfully navigate these wardens, then you finally – and rather underwhelmingly considering the trouble you've gone to – reach the house of Hades itself, a joyless labyrinth of dark, cold halls, surrounded by locked gates.

Charon ferries a soul across the Styx from purgatory to paradise, with hell and its ominous entrance archway in the upper-right quarter, in this sixteenth-century painting of the River Styx by Joachim Patinir.

---

1 While the River Styx is the most commonly identified today, the river navigated by Charon varies between sources. In fact, the majority of ancient Greek writers including Pausanias, Pindar, Euripides and Plato all report Charon as cruising the swamps of the River Acheron. It's the Roman poets, like Propertius, Ovid and Statius, who point to the Styx, perhaps influenced by Virgil's underworld geography in the *Aeneid*.

This sombre picture is emphasised in Homer's *Odyssey*,
when Odysseus visits Hades to consult the seer Tiresias in
Book XI. There he discovers the dulled spirit populous,
unable to communicate with him until revitalised by drinking
the ram's blood he provides them. There is no escape, not
even by suicide, from Hades, a place of punishment, yet not
approaching the severity of some of the more visceral penalties
of Christian hell at its most horrifying. In the *Odyssey*, Homer

describes Tityos's sentence of being stretched out on the ground for two vultures to tear at his liver and bowels forever, in revenge for his violence towards the wife of Zeus; while Tantalus is forced to stand in water up to his chin, which lowers each time he tries to drink it. And there is of course Sisyphus, damned to roll an enormous boulder up a hill, only for it to roll down again the moment he reaches the top.

This colourful mythology, while compelling in narrative terms, was an insufficient eschatology for later philosophers of antiquity. Lucius Annaeus Seneca, for example, the Roman Stoic philosopher who lived at the same time as Jesus, summed up his attitude towards the planes of existence with '*post-mortem nihil est ipsaque mors nihil*' ('After death, nothing; and death itself is nothing'). (Certainly it seems Seneca would have enjoyed the company of George Bernard Shaw, who once wrote: 'What man is capable of the insane self-conceit of believing that an eternity of himself would be tolerable even to himself?') A contemporary epitaph mentioned by the historian Richard Lattimore in *Themes in Greek and Latin Epitaphs* (1942) matches this scepticism:

Wayfarer, do not pass by my epitaph, but stand and listen, and then, when you have learned the truth, proceed. There is no boat in Hades, no ferryman Charon, no Aeacus keeper of the keys, nor any dog named Cerberus. All of us who have died and gone below are

bones and ashes: there is nothing else. What I have told you is true. Now withdraw, wayfarer, so that you will not think that, even though dead, I talk too much.

But perhaps this later Roman attitude is most tidily summed up by the equivalent of the modern RIP commonly found to have been marked on Roman tombs in antiquity: the abbreviation 'n.f. f. n.s. n.c.' – *non fui, fui, non sum, non curo* (I was not. I was. I am not. I care not).

ABOVE: *Detail of a deceased youth from a mixing vessel painted by the artist known as 'the Underworld Painter', an ancient Greek Apulian vase painter whose works date to the second half of the fourth century BC.*

HEL: THE NORSE UNDERWORLD

So many details of the Viking culture disappeared with the breath with which they were spoken: theirs was an oral tradition, their histories maintained by *skalds* (Scandinavian bards who recited the epic poems known as sagas). It wasn't until after their comparatively late and gradual conversion to Christianity that a tradition of manuscript recording began. There was no central Viking church – their communities were scattered, their pantheon of gods many and varied. Therefore, when examining the sagas as principal sources for their afterlife doctrines, we find a complex panoply of notions. In the words of the historian H. R. Ellis Davidson: 'There is no consistent picture in Norse literary tradition of the fate of the dead… to oversimplify the position would be to falsify it.' Despite this, with the additional help of archaeological discoveries, there are principal themes towards attitudes to death, and to some extent afterlife geography, that we can sieve from the disarray.

Henry Wheaton's attempt to map the various plains of existence of Norse mythology, from his History of the Northmen… *(1831). The underworld Niflheim overlaps with the Norse idea of Hel.*

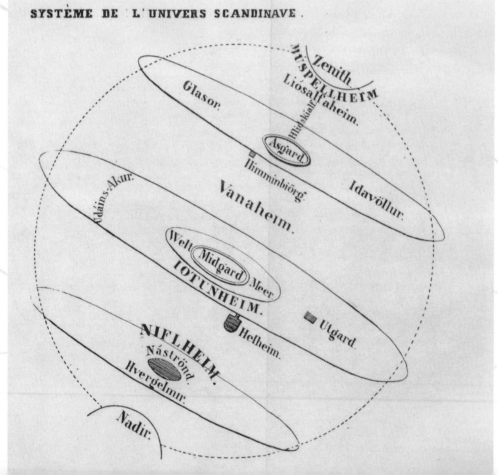

Notably, the principal tenet of reward and punishment for one's moral or ideological choices in life, of salvation and damnation, that underpins so many afterlife beliefs around the globe, was not a notion held by the Norse before the arrival of Christianity. (There is an afterlife of punishment named Náströnd (shore of corpses) mentioned in the poem *Völuspá*, where snakes slither across the floor and poison drips from its ceiling, but the influence of Christianity is clear.)

The most famous of these post-mortem destinations is of course Valhalla, (explored on page 190); but there are other less-known alternatives also believed to receive portions of the dead. The Asgardian goddess of fertility, Freyja, for example, welcomed travelled souls into her own hall, Folkvang (the field of the people, or the field of warriors), but references to this are so sparse that we have no descriptive details.

Occasionally, we find mention of a less pleasant destination: dying at sea carried with it the risk of being dragged down to the underwater kingdom of the giantess Rán. Again, mentions of this fate are scarce, but we know that Rán and her equally enormous husband Ægir lived in their own splendid hall beneath the waves on the ocean floor. Ægir comes across as a generally benevolent type, but Rán is terrifying, a personification of the whimsically lethal seas, and indeed it is she who is blamed for seizing those who fall overboard and pulling them down into her murky depths.

In Norse belief, giants such as Rán are the great nemeses of the gods, and it is this enmity that will one day instigate Ragnarök, a cataclysmic battle between the two sides that the gods were expected to lose. (Although, as with most apocalyptic predictions, when it came to pinning down exactly *when* this would happen details were a little hazy.) Rán and her subaquatic kingdom of the dead had a counterpart in the goddess Hel, unfeeling daughter of Loki and the giantess Angrboða, with her siblings being the monstrous wolf Fenrir and the giant Midgard Serpent. Hel presided over a subterranean netherworld that shared her name. ('Hel' is etymologically related to the Old English 'hell', as both terms derive from the Proto-Germanic feminine noun *xaljō* (concealed place, the underworld) from which we can also trace Valhalla (hall of the slain) and indeed the Modern English word 'hall'.) 'She is half blue-black and half flesh-colour (by which she is easily recognised),' the *Prose Edda* tells us, 'and very lowering and fierce.'

Hermóðr, a son of Odin and messenger of the gods, kneels before Hel to offer a ransom in exchange for his brother Baldr's return, as told in Section 49 of the Prose Edda *book* Gylfaginning.

Of Hel the place, we glean more details from various descriptions in late Icelandic sources of its inhabitants and items with which one was buried to facilitate the final journey. A cold realm of shadow, its citizenry were initially the souls of both the brave and timid, but the mythical place grew to be the destination of those who died in a 'cowardly manner' – i.e. not valiantly in battle, as a bleak contrast to Valhalla. By the thirteenth

An 1859 illustration of Yggdrasil, the Norse world tree that connects the heavens, the material world and the underworld.

BAXTERS Patent Oil Printing 11 Northampton Square

century, Hel was a place akin to Christian hell, of misfortune, pain and punishment. 'Evil men go to Hel,' says Snorri Sturluson, the early thirteenth-century Icelandic historian, 'and thence down to the Misty Hel; and that is down in the ninth world.' He describes Hel's citizenry as shivering, ghostly figures who died ignominious deaths of disease or old age.

According to the Prose Edda book *Grímnismál*, Hel is a great hall located beneath one of the three roots of the world tree Yggdrasil. (Other sources place it in the dark, frozen far north and mention, like Hades of Greek mythology, that Hel's gates are guarded by a savage hound, similar to Cerberus.) 'Her walls are exceeding high and her gates great,' writes Sturluson. 'Her hall is called Sleet-Cold; her dish, Hunger; Famine is her knife; Idler, her thrall; Sloven, her maidservant; Pit of Stumbling, her threshold, by which one enters; Disease, her bed; Gleaming Bale, her bed-hangings.'

Its perimeter is also interesting – the Helvegr (the way to Hel) is ridden by people attempting to cross from the land of the living. Reality is blurred in this hinterland. In the short poem *Helreið Brynhildar* (Brynhild's Hel-Ride), the character Brynhild comes across a dead giantess at her own burial mound, while riding along the Helvegr in an ornate cart in which she was ceremonially burnt in the upper world. In *Baldrs Draumar* (Baldr's Dreams), Odin navigates the Helvegr to reach the underworld to commune with a dead prophetess about his son's visions of his own death.

Hel also has its role to play in the end of the world. It is the crowing of a 'sooty-red cock from the halls of Hel' that will in part herald the beginning events of Ragnarök; but the most dramatic poetry involving Hel comes later in the *Völuspá*. As the time of Ragnarök finally draws near, and the world prepares to be torn asunder by the titanic pyrrhic conflict, the dead of Hel form the crew of a fleet of ghost ships commanded by Loki, who leads them to the battlefield where the final confrontation will take place:

O'er the sea from the north | there sails a ship
With the people of Hel, | at the helm stands Loki;
After the wolf | do wild men follow,
And with them the brother | of Byleist goes.

'Hard does it seem | to the host of the slain', adds the writer of the *Grímnismál*, 'to wade the torrent wild.'

ABOVE: *An illustration of Hermóðr riding to Baldr in Hel, from an Icelandic manuscript of 1760 in the collection of the Royal Danish Library.*

BELOW: *The title page of a manuscript of the* Prose Edda *of Snorri Sturluson, showing Odin, Heimdallr, Sleipnir and other figures from Norse mythology.*

JAHANNAM: ISLAMIC HELL

In the Islamic faith, on dying the soul is taken by Azrael, the Angel of Death, to Barzakh, a kind of limbo plane where the Day of Judgement is awaited. The Qur'an is short on information about this interval between death and resurrection, but later literature emphasises the weighing of virtue – the pious Muslim will experience a peaceful death and an easy journey, but the infidel's soul will be torn from the body and, on failing the questioning and judgement conducted by the angels Munkar and Nakir, will be tormented until taking its place in hell, where the profound torment begins. 'But he whose balance (of good deeds) is found to be light will have his home in a (bottomless) Pit. And what will explain to you what this is? A Fire blazing fiercely!' (Qur'an 101:8-11.)

The alternative is the paradise of Jannah, sometimes referred to simply as 'the Garden', but to get there one must make a perilous journey along the As-Sirāt, the bridge that all dead must walk along to reach paradise. The pious are whisked across by their good deeds, but for the sinner the bridge is said to shrink to the width of a human hair and become as sharp as a razor blade. Down tumbles the sinner, to the fires of hell below.

The hell reserved for misers and the hell of flatterers, from a c.1465 manuscript.

Hell is referred to in the Qur'an as Jahannam or Gehenna, derived from the Hebrew Gey-Hinnom (the valley of Hinnom) – a valley near Jerusalem where, in the Hebrew Bible, some of the kings of Judah performed child sacrifices by fire (see page 78 for more). Jahannam is a place of inextinguishable fire, which according to Islamic tradition is sixty-nine times hotter than the fires on Earth. It is fuelled by the eternal combustion of the sinners themselves. See, for example, the Qur'an verse 2:24: '... fear the Fire whose fuel is men and stones, which is prepared for those who reject Faith'; and 21:98: 'Indeed you and what you worship besides Allah are the firewood of hell...'; and 72:15: 'And as to those who go astray, they are fuel of hell.'

The hell visited by the Prophet Muhammad during his night journey, from a 1436 copy of the Islamic Me'rāj-nāmas (Books of Ascension).

One of the most fascinating physical descriptions of the fire, as Jahannam is sometimes simply known, is given by the Muslim philosopher al-Ghazali (*c.*1058-1111), who incarnates hell in a dramatised account of the final Day of Judgement. In it, Jahannam is a monstrous beast of world-ending size, 'clattering, thundering and moaning' as it lumbers into an attack on humanity. Everyone, even the prophets, fall to their knees in terror. Abraham, Moses and Jesus clutch God's throne in fear as the beast approaches; but Muhammad seizes the beast's bridle, and orders it to retreat until man is ready to enter it.

Qadi Ayyad (1083-1149), a judge of Granada, also portrays the personified Fire in his eschatological work *Daqa`iq al-akhbar fi dhikr al-janna wa-l-nar*. Each of the four legs of the

beast is said to be the size of 'one thousand years' and carries
thirty heads. Each of these heads has 30,000 mouths, each of
these has 30,000 teeth, each as large as a mountain. The lips of
each mouth are pierced with iron chains, made of 70,000 rings.
Each ring carries 'innumerable angels'.

In other Hadiths (collections of traditions containing the
sayings of the prophet Muhammad, which constitute a major
source of guidance for Muslims together with the Qur'an)
further detail is given of Hell the creature. When God
summons the Fire to Him, the Fire 'walks on four legs and is
bound by 70,000 reins. On each of the reins are 70,000 rings;
if all the iron in the world were collected it would not equal
that of one ring. On every ring are 70,000 guardians of hell; if
even one among them were ordered to level the mountains or
to crush the earth he would be able to do it.' Another describes
the sound the Fire emits as being akin to the braying of a
colossal donkey.

As well as the descriptions of hell as a living creature, we
have the detailed geographical depictions of Jahannam as a
netherworld crater of concentric circles composed of these
aforementioned regions on the underside of the flat Earth. One
relevant passage is verse 15:43-44 of the Qur'an: 'And verily,
Hell is the promised abode for them all. It has seven gates: to
each of those gates is a specific class of sinners assigned.'

Qadi Ayyad takes this detail of seven gates farther and
identifies them by name, as well as the infernal department
locked behind each one. The gate to the lowest region of hell,
hawiya (abyss), is reserved for hypocrites and those who take
a flexible approach to truth. The next gate *jahim* (hellfire)
welcomes polytheists. *Saqar* (blaze) is for the Sabians, a
religious group mentioned three times in the Qur'an. For the
Zoroastrians and Satanic worshippers stands the fourth gate
laza (flame), and for the Jews the fifth hell-gate *hutama*. Christians
are designated the sixth gate, *sa-ir* (fire). The seventh gate,
jahannam, beckons Muslims who have committed grave sins.

Those waiting to enter their designated gate have the extra
torture of watching the virtuous pass into paradise, as the
main gates to both hell and heaven are in close proximity, at
the point of the lowest heaven. In fact, the queues stretch past
each other, separated by a wall. This cruel taunt is narrated in
Surah Al-A'raf (7:44-51) of the Qur'an: 'And the companions of
Paradise will call out to the companions of the Fire, "We have

*The punishments of hell,
from* Aḥwāl al-Qiyāma
*(Conditions of Resurrection),
late sixteenth century.*

already found what our Lord promised us to be true. Have you found what your Lord promised to be true?" They will say, "Yes." Then an announcer will announce among them, "The curse of Allah shall be on the wrongdoers." ' On top of this, those who are bound for hell beg the righteous for some of the water provided them by Allah, but are refused.

In both the verses of the Qur'an and the Hadiths, the Fire is presented as the antipode of paradise in both geography and nature, its every feature an extreme opposite. And so, to offset the particular pleasures of paradise, the arsenal of punishments awaiting sinners is most imaginatively developed. The worst of all tortures is the distance from God, the punishment for disbelievers and wrongdoers who realise in their misery that they failed to heed Allah's guidance and cautions, and have brought His wrath on themselves.

Having said that, the agony of the physical tortures certainly comes close to rivalling this absence of divine love. Those who withheld crops for themselves, for example, are forced to carry the sum total of these selfish reserves in a sack on their backs, while those who withheld other forms of alms are tormented by the *zabibatan*, a bald creature who strangles sinners with its prehensile tail. Others are forced to suffer swollen genitals that ooze pus so disgusting that it causes those around them to vomit. Qadi Ayyad repeats descriptions of sinners chased by snakes and scorpions the size of donkeys.

One interesting natural feature of Jahannam is a giant hell-tree named in the Qur'an as Zaqqum (e.g. 56:52: 'you shall eat of a tree called Zaqqum'), which grows from the bottom of hell and which bears fruit in the form of devil-heads. Again, this is a mirror image of a feature of heaven, where the paradise tree Tuba grows amid rivers of gold and silver. (It is also clearly linked to the story of the tree that grows on the mythical island of Wak-Wak, sought by explorers, which grows fruit of screaming human heads, which salute the rising and setting sun.[1]) 'Indeed, the Tree of Zaqqum is food for the sinful, like murky oil, it boils within bellies, like the boiling of scalding water,' goes the verse. 'Verily, the tree of deadly fruit will be the food of the sinful. Like molten lead will it boil in the belly, like the boiling of burning despair.' (Qur'an 44:43-46.)

---

1 For more on this and other mythical features of historical cartography, see Brooke-Hitching, E. (2016) *The Phantom Atlas*, London: Simon & Schuster.

Elsewhere one also finds: 'Is that the better entertainment or the Tree of Zaqqum? For we have truly made it [as] a trial for the wrong-doers. It is a tree that springs out of the bottom of Hell-Fire. The shoots of its fruit-stalks are like the heads of devils. Truly they will eat thereof and fill their bellies therewith. Then on top of that they will be given a mixture made of boiling water. Then shall their return be to the (Blazing) Fire.' (Qur'an 37:62-68.)

We even have an eyewitness description of hell, albeit brief, from Muhammad himself. This is mentioned in one of the Seerah (the traditional Muslim biographies of Muhammad), as part of a version of the 'Night Journey', when *c.*621 the prophet flew from Mecca to Jerusalem in a single night, and ascended to the Seventh Heaven on a winged, horse-like, white beast

The mythical Wak-Wak tree and its human-shaped fruit. From Ta'rikh al-Hind al-Gharbi *(1729).*

called Buraq. In Seerah 268, it's recounted how Gabriel brings Muhammad to the lowest heaven, which is adjacent to the gates of hell. All but one of the angels welcome him with smiles: Maalik, the administrator of hell. Muhammad asks Gabriel to command Maalik to reveal hell to him. Maalik obeys, and removes the covers: 'And the flames blazed high into the air until I thought that they would consume everything.'

Muhammad glimpses the sufferings of sinners: men who stole the wealth of orphans now bear the monstrous lips of camels, stuffing fire into their mouths, flames bursting from their posterior; women who had given birth to bastards were hung by their breasts; and adulterous men who had chased after forbidden women were dining on stinking rotten meat, despite there being fresh meat before them. Having seen all he needs to, Muhammad quickly asks Gabriel to have Maalik seal it back up.

The angel Maalik opens the doors to hell at the request of the Prophet Muhammad during his journey through the afterlife.

FOLLOWING PAGES: *A fabulous composite painting of Buraq, the winged creature that carried Muhammad on his night journey (with its rider Muhammad not depicted), dated to c.1770.*

MESOAMERICAN UNDERWORLDS

The sarcophagus lid of K'inich Janaab' Pakal, seventh-century ajaw (ruler of Palenque), found in the Temple of the Inscriptions, Palenque, Mexico. This astonishingly beautiful afterworld depiction shows Pakal caught between two worlds, tumbling down into the gaping jaws of the underworld while above him is the heavenly muan *bird, atop the Cosmic Tree.*

Today we use the word 'Maya' as a collective term for the pre-Columbian peoples who thrived in the region encompassing the modern territories of southeastern Mexico, Guatemala and Belize, but this was not a term used by the people themselves – nor did they consider themselves to be a unified culture. By 2000 BC, the first agricultural villages had developed; by the Preclassic period (*c.*2000 BC to AD 250) the first complex societies.

The first Maya cities existed by 750 BC, and by 500 BC the monumental architecture and stucco facades for which they are renowned were a common feature.

As well as being admired for their art, architecture, mathematics, calendar and for having the most highly developed of all pre-Columbian writing systems, the Maya also held a complex yet beautiful cosmovision, or model, of the universe. They believed in cycles of regeneration and destruction: the world (which is flat, cornered and rests on the back of a giant cosmic crocodile lying peacefully in a pool of water lilies) has been obliterated four times before, and created five times. Above it sit thirteen heavens, crowned by the divine *muan* bird of heaven, a type of screech-owl.

Below the earth lurk nine layers of underworlds, an idea one can see represented in the nine tiers of the enormous stone pyramids built as tombs for Mayan kings, like the Temple of the Inscriptions at Palenque, Temple I at Tikal and the Pyramid of Kukulcán at Chichen Itza. Each cosmic level was populated by colourful figures from their polytheistic pantheon of at least 166 named gods. The most significant of these gods are the Maker, the Begetter, the Maker of the Blue-Green Plate, and the Sovereign Plumed Serpent, who all play a part in the creation of the Earth. But the most feared are the Lords of the underworld Xibalba (pronounced 'Shee-bal-ba'), as the K'iche' Maya named it, which literally translates to Place of Fright, a subterranean landscape featuring a court of twelve death gods. We learn of this from the *Popol Vuh* (Book of the People), a narrative originally of oral tradition that was transcribed in 1550.

The death gods were known to pop up in the world of the living to spread disease and despair. The two leading figures are One Death and Seven Death, although in the oral tradition of the Lacandon people there is only one chief death god, the skeletal Cizin. The other lower-ranked death gods are pestilential demons who operate in pairs: Flying Scab and Blood Gatherer poison the blood of their victims with illness; Pus Master and Jaundice Demon cause swelling of the body; Bone Sceptre and Skull Sceptre turn corpses into skeletons; Wing and Packstrap cause people to fatally cough up blood while out walking; while Sweepings Demon and Stabbing Demon hide in the dirty areas of homes and wait to stab to death those who are behind on their household chores.

An earthenware Maya vase with three gods of the underworld, made 600-900.

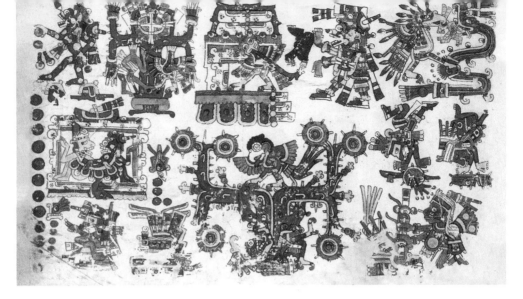

Roamed by demonic predators, Xibalba is a vast land from which there is no escape. The *Popol Vuh* reveals it to be a giant city of deception and trickery – just travelling to its outskirts involved overcoming a series of booby traps. First one has to cross a river of scorpions, then a thick river of blood, then an oozing river of pus. Farther on, the traveller must navigate a crossroads of four roads, which each speak aloud to lead one astray. Finally, the visitor reaches the council place of Xibalba, where protocol dictates he or she must greet the seated Lords. This, however, is a confusing and humiliating process, because the seats around the Lords have been filled with lifelike dummies, making it difficult to know who to approach. The deceased is then offered a bench to rest and recover from the embarrassment, but this seat turns out to be a scalding hot cooking plate.

When the Lords of Xibalba have had enough fun with these humiliations, the deceased is sent for further trials in at least six houses of endurance tests. The Dark House is completely without light; the Rattling House, or Cold House, is kept at sub-zero temperatures with hail ricocheting off its walls; a third is filled with fires and unbearable heat. The Jaguar House is crawling with ravenous jungle cats; another contains swooping, screaming bats; and finally there is the House of Razor Blades in which knives fly around of their own will. There was apparently no Maya spiritual justice system of weighing up merits and virtue – only those who had died an especially violent death avoided being sent there. For everyone else, there was an expectation to undergo this litany of trials, which is why we find the Maya dead buried with post-mortem survival kits of weapons, tools, precious stones, cocoa for sustenance and pet dogs – both real and made of pottery – for companionship.

ABOVE: *Page 52 of the Codex Borgia, depicting Mictlampa, the northern hemisphere of Mictlān, the Aztec underworld. The Codex Borgia is a Mesoamerican ritual and divinatory manuscript believed to have been written before the Spanish conquest of Mexico.*

BELOW: *A cylindrical drinking cup by the Maya vase painter known as the Metropolitan Master, one of the finest existing Maya deity portraits. It features a terrifying death god with skull, extruded eyeballs and distended belly of a corpse.*

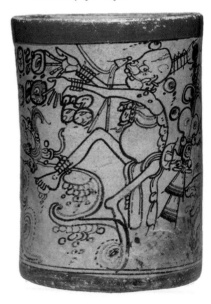

For the Inca civilisation, which grew from the Peruvian highlands sometime in the early thirteenth century until its destruction by the Spanish in 1572, the architecture of the cosmos was of a comparatively simpler design. Though the Inca had no writing system and passed down their mythology orally, details survive of their concept of *pacha* (usually translated as 'world'), which divided the cosmos into three: *hana pacha* (Quechua for 'world above'); *kay pacha* (this world); and the *ukhu pacha* (world below), all places of physical geography where time runs concurrently. These opposites existing in harmony is typical of the interesting Incan philosophy of *yanantin* (complementary dualism), a term still used by modern Andeans and meaning anything that has ever been has existed as a balance of opposing features.

Following the Spanish invasion and subsequent Catholic missionary work, the *hana pacha* was synthesised with the Christian notion of heaven; while its counterpart, *ukhu pacha* (or *urin pacha* in Quechua, *manqhapacha* or *manqhipacha* in Aymara), was tied with the traditional notion of hell. It was ruled over by Supay, the god of death (who would become associated with the Devil), who with his army of demon helpers, also called *supay*, routinely emerged to torture the living. The Inca had their own simple code of conduct to ensure this

Page 53 of the Codex Borgia, showing the Aztec gods of the afterlife, including Xōchipilli (left), the god of art, lust and patron of male prostitutes.

particular afterworld was avoided: *ama suwa*, *ama llulla*, *ama
quella* (do not steal, do not lie, do not be lazy). The deceased
were often mummified by their loved ones and, unusually,
placed in an upright sitting position in preparation for their
journey to the next life. To help them through the trials to be
faced, corpses were buried with items like jugs of water. If one's
heart was eaten or destroyed on Earth, then a more beautiful and
durable object – a precious stone – was put in its place.

Features of these afterworlds are shared among the pre-
Columbian Mesoamerican cultures. Supay, the death gods
One Death and Seven Death of the K'iché, and Cizin of the
Lacandon, all have a counterpart in Aztec tradition in the form
of Mictlāntēcutli, Lord of the underworld known as Mictlān
in the beliefs of the Aztec civilisation, which flourished 1300 to
1521 in the area now known as central Mexico. Mictlān is also
composed of nine levels, and features in the earliest creation
myths of the Aztec.

The plumed serpent deity Quetzalcoatl travels to the
underworld to retrieve bones from which to generate mankind.
He finds Mictlāntēcutli sitting on his throne of the dead,

surrounded by owls and spiders, drinking pus from a human skull. Mictlāntēcutli agrees to hand over the bones on the condition that Quetzalcoatl loudly blow on a conch shell while travelling around Mictlān four times in tribute. The shell he is provided by Mictlāntēcutli, however, has no holes, and so making sound with it is impossible. Quetzalcoatl commands insects to chew through it, and fills the shell with bees. The buzzing tricks Mictlāntēcutli into thinking Quetzalcoatl has somehow succeeded, and he reluctantly gives up the bones. On his way out, however, Quetzalcoatl falls into a pit that Mictlāntēcutli dug as a trap, and some of the bones break into smaller pieces – for the Aztecs, this explained why humans varied in height.

ABOVE: *The Moche civilisation of northern Peru flourished from c.100 to 800. This Moche ceremonial vessel represents a sexually active, living cadaver of the underworld, his exaggerated proportions emphasise his ability to masturbate and produce semen to fertilise the living earth.*

Mictlān was the ultimate destination for the majority of the Aztec deceased, but there were other possible terminuses for a minority of people: warriors who died bravely in battle, and those who died as part of a human sacrifice to the gods, travelled east, to rise with the Sun in its morning ascent. Women who died in childbirth journeyed to the west, to descend with the Sun. Those killed by storms, floods or any other cause of fatality connected to the rain god Tlaloc escaped to a paradise known as Tlālōcān (see page 181).

Perhaps the strangest alternate terminus, though, is Chichiualquauitl, which has been translated as 'Land of the Breast Tree'. There stands the towering titular tree, Chichihuacuauhco, which is covered in human breasts that drip milk. According to the notes of the sixteenth-century Dominican missionary Pedro de los Ríos: 'This was the third place passed through by spirits of this life, to which went only those children who died without having reached the age of reason.' Using the information of the Florentine Codex of the same century, the Mexican anthropologist Miguel León-Portilla suggested that the nursemaid tree is of particular significance, suggesting that the land it grows in is the Tamoanchan, the mythical place of origin of all Mesoamerican cultures.

LEFT: *A Moche 'Sacrificer Scene Bottle', second to fifth century. Here the fanged Moche deity known in modern scholarship as Wrinkle Face stands on a platform holding a* tumi *(ceremonial knife) in his left hand, and in his right hand a severed head.*

BIBLICAL HELL

SHEOL AND GEHENNA

For the afterworld explorer there are two mysterious Hebrew words of particular interest to be found in the Tanakh (Hebrew Bible), the twenty-four books of ancient writings of the Israelites, which formed the basis of the Old Testament and which are believed by the majority of Christians and religious Jews to be the sacred Word of God. These are Sheol and Gehenna.

With Sheol, a word that occurs over sixty times in the Tanakh, the ancient Israelites shared with their Mesopotamian neighbours the idea of an underworld as a collective grave, the place of congregation for all those who had died. Like the Kur netherworld (see page 24), Sheol is a place of darkness and dust. Importantly, critical scholars are unanimous in describing Sheol as in no way resembling what we would today term 'hell'. In fact, as the late scholar of Judaism, Alan Segal, writes: 'There are not any notions of hell and heaven that we can identify in the Hebrew Bible, no obvious judgment and punishment for sinners nor beatific reward for the virtuous' (*Life After Death*, 2004).

Sheol is most commonly compared to the Greek Hades, a dull netherworld of meagre non-existence; though it might in fact more accurately be a synonym for the literal place of burial – i.e. 'the grave', or 'the pit'. While in Second Temple Judaism (*c.*500 BC-AD 70) there emerged the belief in a section of Sheol known as 'Abraham's Bosom', a safe shelter for the righteous,

OPPOSITE: *Peter Paul Rubens's* Fall of the Damned, *painted c.1620. The rebel angels are hurled by the archangel Michael into the abyss, far from the light of God's love.*

BELOW: Christ's Descent into Hell *by a follower of Hieronymus Bosch, in which Christ breaks down the gates of hell to rescue the souls of the virtuous.*

there is a palpable relief to being spared the fate of this destination in the tone of the author of Psalm 86:12-13: 'I will give thanks to you, O Lord my God, with my whole heart… For great is your steadfast love toward me; you have delivered my soul from the depths of Sheol.' And again in Psalm 30:2-3: 'O Lord, my God, I cried to you for help, and you have healed me. O Lord, you brought up my soul from Sheol, restored me to life from among those gone down to the Pit.'

When considered a place, geographically, Sheol is somewhere in the 'depths' of the Earth (Isaiah 7:11), and marks the point at the greatest possible distance from heaven (Job 11:8). Occasionally, the living are thrown down into Sheol before their natural time, at which point the Earth is described as 'opening her mouth' to release them (Numbers 16:30). It is a land, and a place with gates (Job 17:16), with 'farthest corners' (Isaiah 14:15). The dead lead a pale existence there of 'non-life', without knowledge or feeling (Job 14:13), and it is a silent realm of oblivion to those that enter (Psalms 88:13).

Gehenna (or Gehinnom), on the other hand, is believed to be based on a real terrestrial location, a hell one can still visit, a small valley to the south of Jerusalem known as the 'valley of the son of Hinnom'. Here, it was said that, at a specific location called Topheth, the ancient Canaanites made sacrifices to the gods Moloch and Ba'al by burning their own children alive, while beating drums to hide the screams. 'And he defiled Topeth', writes the author of 2 Kings 23:10, 'which is in the valley of the son of Hinnom, that no man might make his son or his daughter to pass through the fire to Molech.'

This led to the area being viewed as a cursed place, and it quickly became a figurative equivalent for hell, and confusingly, in English translations, literally replaced with the word 'hell'. The later tradition of describing Gehenna as a place of judgement and of perpetually burning fire is traced back to the commentary on Psalm 27 by the medieval Provence-born scholar Rabbi David Kimhi (1160-1235), who writes that in this foul valley ever-burning fires were maintained to destroy rubbish, and the cadavers of animals and criminals thrown into it. (There is however no archaeological nor textual evidence to support this burning rubbish dump idea.)

In rabbinic literature, Gehenna is characterised as a destination of the wicked, but in more of a purgatorial sense, where one can leave upon admitting one's past transgressions.

The geography of hell laid out. From a 1596 edition of Hieronymo Natali's Evangelicae historiae imagines, an illustrated guide to the gospels.

It is also enormous, a subterranean abyss that can be reached via the bottom of the ocean, linked to the Earth via a small hole through which its fires burst to heat the Earth's surface. Some rabbinical writers located this hole in the valley of Hinnom, with entrance gates numbering between three to seven, to be found between two palm trees. Some described it as being sixty times larger than Eden (which was also thought by the same writers to be sixty times as large as the world); for others, its size is constantly growing to accommodate new inhabitants. The longest sentence a Jew will endure in Gehenna is eleven

Michelangelo's The Last Judgement *fresco in the Sistine Chapel, painted between 1536 and 1541. The figure of Christ dominates the scene as the verdict of the Last Judgement is brought.*

months (unless one is a creature of pure wickedness, in which case it's twelve months). Quite a different place to the underworld of Sheol / Hades, then – although you'd be hard-pushed to find either in the King James Version of the Bible, which translates these terms with the Anglo-Saxon word *hell*.

Nowhere in the Tanakh (or Old Testament) can we find the traditional Christian view of the afterlife. For the ancient Israelites, death was effectively the end of the story; but towards the very end of the Old Testament period, and certainly by the time of the historical Jesus, Jewish thinking had come to form the ideas of a last Day of Judgement and resurrection (possibly, it is thought, under the influence of the dualistic Zoroastrianism – although, as the scholar Bart D. Ehrman points out in *Heaven and Hell*, 2020, it is not entirely clear who influenced whom).

At the end of time, when the events of human history had played out, God would bring back to life both the righteous and sinful in their physical bodies. The righteous would live forever in peaceful bliss in the perfect utopian kingdom that God had established on Earth, while the wicked would be shown their crimes and then be obliterated from all plains of existence forever. This is almost certainly the view of the historical Jesus and his earliest followers, who did not appear to believe that, on dying, a person's soul went to heaven or hell. This coming Kingdom of God on Earth was at the heart of Jesus's teachings: 'The time has been fulfilled,' go his first recorded words in the opening lines of the oldest Gospel, 'the Kingdom of God is at hand. Repent and believe the good news.' (Mark 1:15.)

Following Jesus's death, his disciples continued proclaiming his message, even as they transformed it – for the end he had predicted had not come. Thus, his message had to be re-evaluated, and it came to be believed that, instead of a grand ushering into eternity at the end of time, this fate awaited each person shortly after their individual point of death; and the idea of punishment and reward transformed into separate realms rather than, as Jesus had spoken of, a Kingdom of God on Earth and eventual annihilation of the wicked. Gradually, over centuries, the realm of hell was constructed in popular thought.

The word 'hell' does not appear in the Greek New Testament; instead one of three words is used: the Greek words Tartarus or Hades, or the Hebrew word Gehinnom. So what details of these places does the New Testament give us? Matthew 5:22 warns of the 'danger of hell fire' as punishment, an 'everlasting

An eighteenth-century depiction of a sacrificial statue of Moloch, with a fire at the base and seven chambers for child sacrifice in the torso. From a 1738 edition of Johann Lund's Die alten jüdischen Heiligthümer.

fire' that should be avoided at all costs: 'And if thine eye offend thee, pluck it out, and cast it from thee: it is better for thee to enter into life with one eye, rather than having two eyes to be cast into hell fire' (Matthew 18:9). In Matthew 22:13, it is an 'outer darkness, there shall be weeping and gnashing of teeth'; the author of Jude 1:13 writes of 'wandering stars, to whom is reserved the blackness of darkness for ever'.

But by far the most visual descriptions are those provided in the prophetic visions in Revelation, the only apocalyptic book in the New Testament canon, by an author who names himself as 'John', who modern scholars identify as John of Patmos,[1] a Greek island, writing in the reign of the Roman emperor and anti-Christian persecutor Domitian (AD 81-96). With extraordinary imagery the book presents a dramatic cosmic battle between the forces of good and evil, with the appearance of enormous beasts. A great dragon (with seven heads, ten horns and seven crowns on his heads) snares a third of the stars of heaven with his enormous tail, and sends them tumbling to the earth (Revelation 12:3-4). Then: 'I stood upon the sand of the sea, and saw a beast rise up out of the sea, having seven heads and ten horns, and upon his horns ten crowns, and upon his heads the name of blasphemy' (Revelation 13:1) This beast of the sea is followed by another similarly titanic creature of land. (The beast from the sea has been interpreted as symbolising the Roman Empire with its city of seven hills, while the beast from the earth is generally identified with the Roman imperial cult.)

In Chapter 20, the pit of hell is mentioned, for example: 'And I saw an angel come down from heaven, having the key of the bottomless pit and a great chain in his hand… And he laid hold on the dragon, that old serpent, which is the Devil, and Satan, and bound him a thousand years, and cast him into the bottomless pit, and shut him up, and set a seal upon him, that he should deceive the nations no more, till the thousand years should be fulfilled' (Revelation 20:1-3).

This is followed shortly by verse 10, which describes how 'the devil that deceived them was cast into the lake of fire and brimstone, where the beast and the false prophet are, and shall be tormented day and night for ever and ever'. Revelation also describes how any whose name are not found written in the

---

1 It is a curious quirk that Revelation, which claims to have been written by someone named John, is not called the book of John; while the Fourth Gospel is called John, despite its author being anonymous, identifying themselves only as a 'disciple whom Jesus loved'.

LEFT AND OPPOSITE: *Between 1805 and 1810 William Blake was commissioned to produce over one hundred paintings to illustrate books of the Bible. Shown here are works inspired by the Revelation: Left:* The Great Red Dragon and the Woman Clothed with the Sun. *Right:* The Great Red Dragon and the Beast from the Sea.

Book of Life are thrown into the lake of fire, along with Death and Hades themselves, who are also thrown into the burning lake. Following this banishment of death and hell, the Kingdom of God descends to Earth:

And I saw a new heaven and a new earth: for the first heaven and the first earth were passed away; and there was no more sea. And I John saw the holy city, new Jerusalem, coming down from God out of heaven, prepared as a bride adorned for her husband. And I heard a great voice out of heaven saying, Behold, the tabernacle of God is with men, and he will dwell with them, and they shall be his people, and God himself shall be with them, and be their God.

Revelation 21:1-3

Like Jesus, the author of Revelation believes the wicked would be exterminated, never to live again; but Revelation's lake of fire would be one of many such infernal details turned into the fiery pits of hell for sinners to burn in for all eternity.

FOLLOWING PAGES: The Woman and the Beast, *from the magnificent* Silos Apocalypse *(c.1100) showing Revelation's war in heaven, woman clothed in the sun with the moon at her feet (top left) and the attack of the seven-headed dragon.*

VISIONS AND TOURS OF HELL

Further details on the developing Christian image of hell can be found in the Apocrypha – writings by early Christians that fall outside the traditionally established canon of biblical books, usually due to dubious origin. Apocalyptic literature of the first few Christian centuries gave colourfully disastrous predictions of Judgement Day, and the state of afterlife that would ensue, purporting to have been written by the famous apostles, saints and other prominent biblical figures. Take for example the fourth-century *Apocalypse of Paul* – in its preface, its scribe claims to have discovered the original manuscript written by Paul buried in a marble case, together with the apostle's own shoes.

Holy shoeboxes aside, the forger mainly betrays themselves by stating the date of this 'discovery' as 388. This caused great confusion among medieval scholars, who had found references to Paul in works written more than 150 years before this date. In his *Apocalypse*, 'Paul' describes a hell of rivers erupting in flames, a reeking pit for infidels located on the north side of hell, and deadly snowfalls in freezing temperatures that fill the air with the sound of chattering teeth. There are extraordinary amounts of blood, worms (the worst of which, 'the one that does not sleep', lies in the north-side pit), animals and avenging angels with torture instruments. The last are led by Tartaruchus (keeper of Tartarus), the angel of torments, head-torturer and supervisor of the Day of Judgement. Each soul, it is revealed, has its own angel who keeps a record of its sins, although God states that only immoral acts committed in the last five years are of relevance.

In the grim *Apocalypse of Peter*, written earlier, in the mid-second century, crude horrors abound, which would have appealed to the members of the then-persecuted sect, reassured by the promise of gruesome post-mortem revenge on their oppressors. Having shown St Peter the paradise kingdom of the virtuous, Christ guides him around an opposing realm of darkness, where offenders are tortured by angels in black robes, where blasphemers are suspended by their tongues over flames and others drown in a flaming lake. Female adulterers are dangled by their hair over boiling dung, while unfaithful males hang upside down with heads submerged in the filth. Murderers are covered in hungry worms and are attacked by evil beings, for the amusement of the souls of their murdered victims, who watch and cheer God's justice. Loan sharks are dumped in swamps of pus and blood,

OPPOSITE: *A gorgeous miniature painted by the three Limbourg brothers c.1416 for the* Très Riches Heures *(a Book of Hours) made for the Duke of Berry. In Tundal's hell, the Devil lies on a large grill, exhaling souls upwards with his burning breath.*

FOLLOWING PAGES: *Hidden away at the back of St Peter and St Paul's Church, Chaldon, Surrey is a breathtaking 17ft- (5.2m-) wide 'doom mural' showing busy scenes of both heaven and hell, which dates back to the twelfth century.*

and children who disobeyed their parents are pecked to pieces by carnivorous birds. Those who dabbled in sorcery are nailed to spinning, burning wheels. All cry for God's mercy, which only encourages Tarturachus to intensify their suffering, for it is too late to repent. These metaphysical fires are tortures to be feared because, as theologians of this early medieval period, like St Augustine (354-430), Pope Gregory I (c.540-604) and Julian of Toledo (642-690) all wrote, the soul has a physical being in the afterlife: 'a bodily semblance', as Julian describes it, that means it can experience both peace and tremendous pain.

Visions and tours were not just the preserve of apocryphal saints. In his *History of the Franks*, Gregory of Tours reports the hell vision of Sunniulf, Abbot of Randau, using the image of hell as a giant beehive of sinners: 'He used himself to tell how once he was shown in a vision a certain river of fire, into which men, assembling together on one part of the bank, were plunging like so many bees entering a hive.' The vision served its cautionary purpose. Gregory reports that then 'Sunniulf awoke. From then on he was more severe with his monks.'

To add to this are the visions of an Irish preacher named Fursey, relayed by the Venerable Bede (c.673-735). In one vision, Fursey is flown by angels above a dark valley, towards four giant fires floating in the air. These, he is told, are punishments for, respectively, liars, the covetous, creators of strife and discord, and the pitiless and fraudulent. The four fires joined as one, and Fursey glimpsed devils among the flames, one of whom hurled a tortured sinner directly at him, striking Fursey in the face. When he returned to his body following the vision, the preacher reportedly awoke to find a burn mark from this collision on his jaw and shoulder, which he carried with him for the rest of his life. (Bede adds credibility to Fursey by adding that he could tell the story on a cold winter's day wearing only a thin garment yet still sweat.)

By the 1100s, hell visions had become a distinct literary genre popular with clerics and laymen. The blockbusting title in this field was *Visio Tnugdali* (The Vision of Tundal), a magnificent afterworld journey written c.1149 by an Irish itinerant monk named Brother Marcus, who claims to have heard the story straight from the knight Tundal himself. Having fallen unconscious at the dinner table, the likeable Tundal spends three days in the infernal realm, sent to hell for having spent his money on 'clowns, jesters and minstrels' instead of donating it to the church.

His guardian angel leads him on a tour, showing him murderers cooking on an iron grate over hot coals, as well as a mountain with a fiery slope on one side and a snowy slope on the other, with hailstorms in between, where demons with iron hooks and forks herd the damned from one torture to the next. Tundal himself must tread a thin plank 1000ft (300m) long (another adaptation of the ancient Chinvat bridge) to reach the great beast Acheron, who has eyes of fire and two devils in his mouth like pillars. The angel flees and Tundal finds himself thrown into the colossal creature's belly, but is finally rescued by the angel. The tour resumes: Tundal finds a lake filled with ravenous animals the size of his hand and studded with spikes, then encounters an enormous bird with an iron beak that feeds on promiscuous nuns and priests, excreting their remains into a frozen lake where men and women give birth to snakes. Finally, as demons buzz like bees around him singing 'the song of death', Tundal reaches Lucifer:

Blacker than a crow and shaped like a man except that it had a beak and a spiky tail and thousands of hands, each of which had twenty fingers with fingernails longer than knights' lances, with feet and toenails much the same, and all of them squeezing unhappy souls. He lay bound with chains on an iron gridiron above a bed of fiery coals. Around him were a great throng of demons. And whenever he exhaled he ejected the squeezed unhappy souls upward into hell's torments. And when he inhaled, he sucked them back in to chew them up again.

(See page 85 for an illustration of this scene.) Tundal eventually awakes, to find himself 'clothed in his own body'. With such imagery the story was phenomenally popular – a variety of nearly 250 separate illuminated manuscript copies of the story survive, written in at least fifteen languages.

One last entry to include in the genre of medieval hell tours is *The Vision of Thurkill* (1206), which tells the story of the English ditch-digging peasant Thurkill who is whisked away for a tour of the Other World by St Julian. Thurkill sees spirits covered in black-and-white spots in a landscape of features by now familiar to us: fires, swamps, a spiked bridge, furnaces, a pit and a weighted scale for measuring virtue. But Thurkill also sees in hell an arena with tiered seating, where a spiritual 'multitude' are tied in place with white-hot iron hoops and nails. Devils fill other seats like a night at the theatre, enjoying torture after torture staged for their entertainment.

INTO THE HELL-MOUTH

The hell-mouth is a traditional medieval depiction of a terrifying doorway to Satan's subterranean kingdom in the form of a giant animal's maw, from which tortured souls and demons reach out in agony. A graphic warning of the consequences of leading an un-Christian life, it synthesises four main biblical images: the open pit of hell swallowing sinners; Satan the lion roaming for souls to devour; Satan as a fire-breathing dragon; and Leviathan, the great sea monster of the Old Testament. The image appears to originate from the Anglo-Saxon period, and is even sometimes described as the mouth of the Devil himself: 'Came they never out of the pit of snakes', writes the author of Homily 4:46-8 in the late tenth-century *Vercelli Book*, 'and of the throat of the dragon which is called Satan.'

ABOVE: *Tundal is shown the beast Acheron, illustrated by Simon Marmion in a c.1470 copy of* The Vision of Tundal.

OPPOSITE: *The mouth of hell from* The Hours of Catherine of Cleves *(1440), the greatest surviving Dutch illuminated manuscript.*

RIGHT: *The archangel Michael locks the hell-mouth, in this miniature from the Winchester Psalter of the mid-twelfth century.*

A BRIEF HISTORY OF THE DEVIL

Lucifer (from Latin *lux* + *fer* 'light-bearing'), Satan (from Hebrew 'adversary'), Moloch, Beelzebub (from the Hebrew *Ba'al Zəvûv* 'lord of the flies'), the Prince of Darkness, Mephistopheles, the Antichrist, the Father of Lies – the Devil (from Greek *diabolos*, 'slanderer' or 'accuser') has few rivals in the sheer quantity of names he enjoys – with the exception, perhaps, of the English writer and spy Daniel Defoe (born Daniel Foe), who holds the record for most writer's pseudonyms, an estimated 198.[1] Defoe, the son of Presbyterian dissenters, also harboured an obsession with the Devil. In 1726, he published *The Political History of the Devil* in which he exhibits a belief in the physical existence of Satan and his active manipulation of world events throughout history, including the Crusades, and considers him a close associate of Europe's Catholic authorities – which of course earned his book an instant ban by the Roman Catholic Church.

Such preoccupation with the existence of evil, and its personification, has gripped mankind since prehistory. From the beginning, the philosophical problem was always the same – how could one explain the existence of both good and evil in the world? Why would an omnipotent, benevolent god allow the existence of evil? In so many belief systems around the world, the rationale in solving this problem runs the same – there must be two opposing forces of good and evil, raging in perpetual battle. Or, in the rules of storytelling: every protagonist needs an antagonist. Enter the Devil.

In the Middle Ages, Jews, Muslims and Christians all shared a belief in the existence of the Devil in a variety of bestial forms. In Western Europe, manuscript artists took influence from the story of the snake in the Garden of Eden and adorned him with serpentine features, but this chimeric mix of human and bestial traits can be traced back to influences from much earlier religions. In particular, there are the ancient Egyptian figures like Apep (or Apophis),[2] the deity of evil in

An eighth-century BC bronze statuette of Pazuzu, the ancient Mesopotamian king of the demons of the wind. The roots of the Christian image of the Devil trace back to the chimeric gods and demons of the ancient world, from Egypt to Mesopotamia.

---

1 These include Betty Blueskin, Boatswain Trinkolo, Count Kidney Face and Sir Fopling Tittle-Tattle.

2 Rather worryingly, Apophis is soon due to make a return to Earth. On Friday, 13 April 2029, the enormous asteroid is expected to narrowly pass by within 19,000 miles (31,000km) of Earth's surface. A flyby of an object of this scale occurs only every thousand years or so.

Egyptian mythology, chaos and opponent of light, who routinely attacked the barge of the sun god Ra as he sailed through the night. Apep is usually depicted in art of the Middle Kingdom in serpentine form, and is associated with all terrifying natural phenomena like earthquakes and thunderstorms. The ancient Babylonians had winged humanoid demons called lilitu, which terrorised the living at night, seducing men and slaying pregnant women and young children.

As Christianity took hold in the Roman world, worshippers were required to reject all previous, pagan gods as evil spirits. Perhaps the best known of these is Pan, the god of the wild in ancient Greek mythology (with his Roman counterpart being Faunus), half-goat and half-man, with sinfully carnal appetites, goat horns and cloven hooves – characteristics that might sound devilishly familiar.

'I see his cloven foot and saucer eyes!' A plate from the later illustrated edition of Defoe's The Political History of the Devil, *1819.*

The character of personified evil varies in significance from religion to religion. In Judaism, for example, Satan is not a particularly significant figure. Demonic characters do appear on occasion in Hebrew scripture, but the most famous appearance is found in the Book of Job, when an 'adversary' or 'tempter' questions whether Job would continue to praise God if he had his family and every possession torn from him, a test that God duly conducts. God is shown to be the powerful figure in the story, but the fact that the adversary is able to provoke such an action shows that, while not a rival, he is not of insignificant power.

An illustration from Jacobus de Teramo's c.1382 Book of Belial, which takes the form of a lawsuit filed by Lucifer and the forces of hell against Jesus Christ, in which the Devil accuses the Son of God of trespassing into hell, and is suing for damages. Here, the Devil returns to hell, triumphantly waving the writ of his lawsuit.

In Genesis, the serpent who tempts Eve is strongly associated with Satan, but many theologians consider Genesis to predate the idea of the Devil. When the Devil appears in the gospels, tempting (or by another translation, 'testing') Jesus in the desert for forty days and nights as recounted in Matthew 4:1-11, Mark 1:12-13 and Luke 4:1-13 (but not John), it is without any previous explanation of his origins, nor any descriptive detail of his appearance. The First Epistle of Peter warns of this soul-hunter: 'Discipline yourselves, keep alert. Like a roaring lion your adversary the Devil prowls around, looking for someone to devour.' (1 Peter 5:8.) By Revelation, Satan has explosively mutated into an apocalyptic monster, set on overthrowing God and heaven.

William Blake's The Great Red Dragon and Woman Clothed with the Sun.

Lucifer is one name for this inveterate enemy of God and prince of evil spirits, but in fact one could also ask – which Lucifer? A number of figures have been labelled *lucifer* in its original Latin meaning of 'light-bearing'. Originally, it was applied to the planet Venus, the brilliant star of the morning. In the Vulgate Bible, the Latin edition translated by St Jerome at the request of Pope Damasus in 382, Jerome uses *lucifer* for the light of the morning in Job 11:17, as well as the signs of the zodiac in Job 38:32, and for the aurora in Psalm 109:3. In Isaiah 14:12, one finds the word applied metaphorically to the king of Babylon for having fallen from heaven and outshining his contemporaries; to the high priest Simon, son of Onias, for his dazzling virtue (Ecclesiastes 50:6); and to the splendid glory of heaven (Revelation 2:28). Even Jesus Christ himself, as the true light of spiritual guidance, is referred to as *lucifer* in 2 Peter 1:19, Revelation 22:16, and in the lengthy proclamation known as the *Exultet* traditionally sung on the Holy Saturday of Easter.

But it's that metaphorical reference of Isaiah 14:12 that proves crucial in developing the later European Christian notion of the Devil, as writers of the fifth century began to

The angel in blue shown here beside Jesus is thought to be the earliest surviving depiction of the Devil in Christian art, from a sixth-century mosaic in the Basilica Sant'Apollinare Nuovo in Ravenna, Italy.

A bestial Satan, painted by
Francesco Traini, at the
Camposanto Monumentale
(walled cemetery) in Pisa
achieves a kind of
grotesque beauty.

synthesise the Vulgate term for Isaiah's Lucifer with the rebel
angel leader in Revelation, who was cast down from heaven
into the pit with his condemned forces, uniting the adversary
of the Old Testament with the diabolic beast of Revelation.

It was during the Middle Ages that the Devil is bestowed
with his demonic appearance in art, but there are suggestions
that this was not always the popular image. In the Basilica of
Sant'Apollinare Nuovo in Ravenna, Italy, for example, there is
a fascinating sixth-century mosaic (shown opposite) of the Last
Judgement which, it is claimed, shows the earliest surviving
depiction of Satan, who appears as an ethereal blue angel no
less beautiful than Jesus and the angel of God beside him.

Later artists, like Hieronymus Bosch, Albrecht Dürer and
Hendrick Goltzius (to sample just the German canon), who
wanted to fully represent Satan in all his monstrosity, found they

had little in the way of descriptive detail from biblical sources to work with. And so they assembled a hodgepodge of imagery from older traditions and their own imaginations – into this mixing pot went Pan's cloven feet, the horns of eastern cult deities, the snake- and bat-like features of Near Eastern gods and demons, and any other psychologically unsettling motifs.

Artists like Giotto and Fra Angelico often depicted the Devil in their paintings of the Last Judgement under Dantean influence, as a ravenous giant positioned at the core of hell, cheerfully chewing on the souls of traitors. In fact, in terms of literary influences on the representation of Lucifer in the Middle Ages, no work exceeded the impact of the *Inferno* of the fourteenth century, with its graphic descriptions of the dark, three-faced creature lurking in the innermost circle of hell. 'At every mouth he with his teeth was crunching / A sinner... / So that the three of them tormented thus.' Satan bears 'mighty wings... / No feathers had they, but as of a bat.'

The Devil from an English manuscript of c.1327-1335 known as the Holkham Bible Picture Book.

As the image of the Devil developed, so too did his role in everyday life, evolving into the active agent of chaos so feared by Defoe. As Europe suffered the devastations of the Black Death, famine and war, his malignant influence in the torment of the souls of the living was clear for all to see, now not so much a trickster of whom to be wary, but an irresistible corrupter. He was the terror at the heart of the witch-hunt hysteria – women, being weaker and less intelligent than men, as it was thought, were therefore more vulnerable to Satanic persuasion to collude against God's kingdom.

In the sixteenth century, the robust literalism about hell and its ruler gave way to a curiosity as to how it all could be explained in natural terms, and artistic portrayals of Satan gradually shifted from the horrifying monster to a more romantic human figure. The Puritan poet John Milton

LEFT: *The Devil sells indulgences, from the Jena Codex, c.1490-1510, a beautifully illuminated Hussite manuscript from the late Middle Ages.*

FOLLOWING PAGE LEFT: *Lucifer (c.1590-c.1600, Italy) by the printmaker Cornelis Galle the Elder. The figures of Dante and Virgilius (marked D and V) are shown in three separate places: hurrying past him on the ice surface; diving down through the sphere of floating souls, past the demonic genitals that form the centre of the world (a discovery that certainly would have livened up Jules Verne's* Journey to the Centre of the Earth*); and inspecting his feet in the cave at the bottom.* RIGHT: *The Devil devouring the limbs of sinners, from the* Compendium of Demonology and Magic *(c.1775), a magnificent occult manuscript in the collection of the Wellcome Library, London.*

Der fürst der finsternis: Dagol:

Below: Le génie du mal *(The Genius of Evil), a white marble sculpture known informally in English as The Lucifer of Liège, by the Belgian artist Guillaume Geefs (1805-1883), housed in the cathédrale Saint-Paul, Liège, Belgium.*

crowned this character development with arguably the first psychologically engrossing characterisation of the Devil in *Paradise Lost* (1667), who is, at first, not the reptilian predator but more of a strutting, seductive hero. Outwardly, only the lightning scar on his face betrays the evil within. Just as Milton grandly builds up his antihero – 'he above the rest / In shape and gesture proudly eminent / Stood like a tow'r' – he then reveals him to be a failed, embittered idealist seeking revenge, powered by 'dismay mixt with obdurate pride and steadfast hate'.

Thomas Stothard's later painting *Satan Summoning His Legions* of 1790 reveals the continuation of this Miltonian trend of Satan as a tragic figure of pity, when it was popular to purge the more superstitious elements of religion. By the nineteenth century, the Devil was regaining his cunning trickster's identity – see Goethe's Mephistopheles in *Faust*, and Mark Twain's *Mysterious Stranger* – and once more he is, metaphorically, the reptilian personality relying on dark allure and deception,

THE JUDGE.

"TO BEGIN WITH, 'I'LL PAINT THE TOWN RED'."

LEFT: *An American cartoon from 1885 portraying 'Democracy' as the Devil overlooking Washington, DC, holding a bucket labelled 'Bourbon Principles' and a paintbrush (in which appears a profile caricature of Grover Cleveland), both dripping red paint with which he plans to 'paint the town'.*

BELOW: *A purported late-eighteenth-century Polish portrait of the Antichrist.*

rather than the hammer of medieval terror. It is this form that is perhaps closest to his characterisation in modern popular culture, in everything from television shows like *The Twilight Zone* (1959-1964) to films like *Angel Heart* (1987) – for what could better symbolise the insidious mundanity of evil and man's capacity for it, than for its personification to be in our own image?[3]

---

3 Incidentally, both God and the Devil have been the recipients of real lawsuits in recent history. *United States ex rel. Gerald Mayo v. Satan and His Staff*, for example, was filed in 1971 by Gerald Mayo, an inmate at Western Penitentiary, Pittsburgh, who complained that Satan had 'deprived him of his constitutional rights' – it was dismissed after the court noted that as a foreign prince Satan could claim sovereign immunity. In 1970, Arizona lawyer Russel T. Tansie sued God for $100,000 for 'negligence' on behalf of his secretary, Betty Penrose, whose house had been damaged by lightning. When the defendant 'failed to turn up in court', Penrose won the case by default.

DANTE'S *INFERNO* AND THE MAPPING OF HELL

In the construction of the Western image of hell, there is no more significant a figure than Dante Alighieri. The Florentine poet's 14,233-line narrative poem *La divina commedia* (The Divine Comedy), written between *c.*1308 and 1320, envisioned the afterlife with such persuasive, horrific detail that it profoundly shaped the mortal fears of an entire continent, establishing Tuscan as the standardised Italian language, and inspiring the great Western Renaissance artists in the creation of divine masterpieces.

On a vision journey guided by the classical poet Virgil, Dante must travel down through nine tiers of concentric circle hells of sinners, witnessing their torments – from the circles of the lustful and gluttonous to the lower levels of the heretics and traitors – in Book 1, the *Inferno*, before explorations of purgatory and paradise can be embarked on.

'I found myself, in truth, on the brink of the valley of the sad abyss', writes Dante on entering the first circle of hell, Limbo, 'that gathers the thunder of an infinite howling. It was so dark,

Satan by Coppo di Marcovaldo (c.1225-c.1276), for the mosaic ceiling in the Florence Baptistery, Italy around fifty years before Dante produced his Inferno, *likely influencing the poet's three-headed figure (an inversion of the Holy Trinity).*

and deep, and clouded, that I could see nothing by staring into its depths.' Here can be found the unbaptised and virtuous pagans, who, despite not accepting Christ, are not sinful enough to incur damnation.

The Second Circle, Lust, is 'a part where no thing gleams', and is home to, among others, Cleopatra, Helen of Troy, Paris and Achilles. The Third Circle is Gluttony, where sinners wallow in a sucking mire of putrid matter, and are prone to being mauled by the three-headed hellhound Cerberus. Canto VII tells of the Fourth Circle, Greed, where Dante saw how the inhabitants 'strained their chests against enormous weights, and with mad howls rolled them at one another. Then in haste they rolled them back, one party shouting out: "Why do you hoard?" and the other: "Why do you waste?" ' Their infernal journey through further circles culminates with Dante reaching the ninth and lowest circle of hell at the centre of the Earth, where Satan is discovered (referred to by Virgil as 'Dis'), trapped in the ice of Lake Cocytus up to his waist, eternally devouring the great traitors to God: Judas, Brutus and Cassius:

... he had three faces: one in front bloodred;
and then another two that, just above
the midpoint of each shoulder, joined the first;
and at the crown, all three were reattached;
the right looked somewhat yellow, somewhat white;
the left in its appearance was like those
who come from where the Nile, descending, flows.

Inferno, XXXIV, 39-45

The lake is replenished by Lucifer's tears, and frozen by the flapping of his wings as he tries to escape.

As one of the greatest works of literature ever committed to paper, the artistic supremacy of Dante's *Divine Comedy* has influenced writers and artists for centuries with undiminished potency; but his work, and in particular the architectural ingenuity of his hell design, also catalysed an altogether more eccentric artistic and scientific preoccupation: 'infernal cartography', or the mapping of hell.

The hell featured in Dante's poem is a physical, subterranean part of Earth. Situated directly beneath Jerusalem, it takes the form of a giant cone reduced in diameter as it descends towards the centre of the Earth. With such detailed physical description, and the renewed fifteenth-century interest in cartography, it was only a matter of time before the Renaissance obsession with practical measurement was turned towards this, the most potent topographical imagery in contemporary imagination.

Dantean cartography is thought to have been first undertaken by Antonio Manetti, a Florentine mathematician and architect, who believed it possible to map out the precise size, shape and location of Dante's hell. Though he never published his infernal calculations and accompanying maps himself, one of the earliest edited printings of *The Divine Comedy*, produced in 1506 by two significant figures of the Florentine Renaissance, Cristoforo Landino and Girolamo Benivieni, included Manetti's work.

A cartographic trend was born, and infernal cartography flourished among Florentine and Tuscan thinkers throughout the Renaissance, even capturing the imagination of a young

LEFT AND OPPOSITE: *Illustrations by Priamo della Quercia in an Italian manuscript of Dante's* Divine Comedy *created 125 years or so after Dante produced his poem in 1320.* LEFT TOP: *Dante is rowed by Charon across the River Acheron;* LEFT BOTTOM: *Dante and Virgil looking into the tomb of Pope Anastasius II, and the three tiers of the violent;* OPPOSITE TOP: *Virgil and Dante entering the eighth circle of adulterers, seducers and flatterers;* OPPOSITE BOTTOM: *Dante and Virgil witness the punishment of the barterers.*

Galileo Galilei who, in an under-reported episode of his biography, accepted the invitation of the Florentine Academy to deliver two lectures in 1588 on the topography of Dante's hell. Not only did Galileo conclude in favour of Manetti, but we also have the bizarre story of how he, one of the most significant figures of the Scientific Revolution, embarked on his own attempt to structurally engineer hell, producing his own calculations as supporting evidence.

The transcripts of Galileo's two lectures, which remain a fascinating read, reveal the basis of his calculations to be, among other sources of information, Dante's line: 'Already the Sun was joined to the horizon, whose meridian circle covers Jerusalem with its highest point.' Galileo interpreted this to mean that hell's upper diameter must be equal to the radius of the Earth. Accordingly, he calculated that the physical boundary of hell's roof must run from beneath Marseille, France, on the western side, stretching across to Tashkent in modern Uzbekistan to the east. To calculate the thickness of

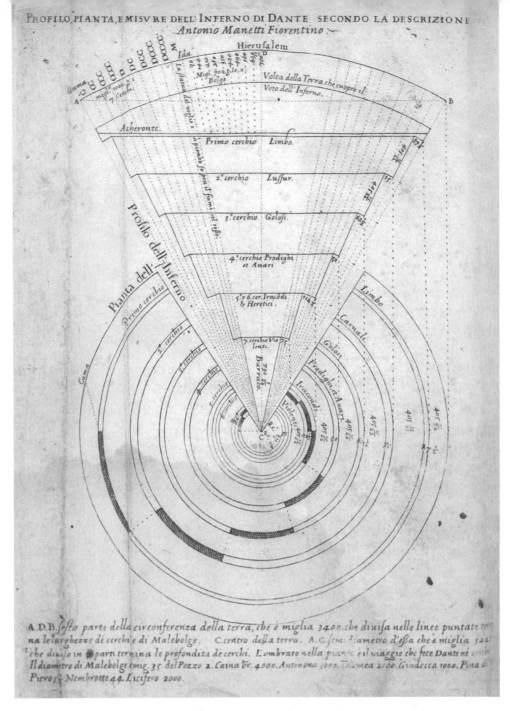

PROFILO, PIANTA, E MISVRE DELL' INFERNO DI DANTE SECONDO LA DESCRIZIONE
Antonio Manetti Fiorentino :~

hell's roof, Galileo based his figures on Brunelleschi's famous design of the duomo in Florence. At 148ft (45m) wide but of a thickness of only 10ft (3m), this suggested that hell's great dome would therefore be 370 miles (600km) thick. (It was only much later that Galileo realised that his own calculations, along with the estimations of others, were fatally flawed – that all those below this giant hell dome would be crushed under its impossible weight.)

Section, Plan and Dimensions of Dante's Inferno, *Antonio Manetti, c.1529.*

LEFT: *Dante's design of the circles of hell was a direct inversion of the belief at that time of the universe consisting of concentric circles of heavenly crystal spheres, each one bearing one of the planets, with Earth at the centre. This illustration from a 1464 manuscript by Gossuin de Metz shows hell at the centre of the universe.*

BELOW: *Maps of Dante's hell by the Florentine architect Antonio Manetti, 1506.*

Giovanni da Modena, The Inferno *(detail), 1410, in the Basilica di San Petronio, Bologna, Italy. Commissioned in Bartolomeo Bolognini's will of 1408, with the stipulation that the* Inferno *painting should be 'as horrible as possible'.*

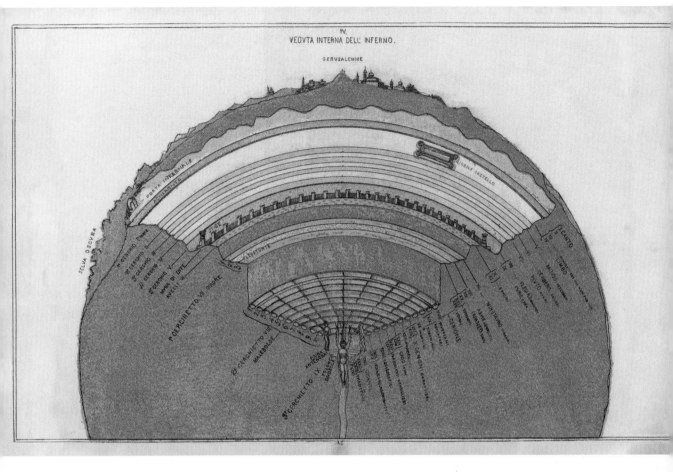

Sandro Botticelli, a Florentine like Manetti, also embarked on his own visual interpretation of Dante's writing to produce what is probably the best-known image of the Inferno (see pages 114-115), the intricately detailed *Map of Hell*, one of ninety paintings he created between the 1480s and 1490s as part of a commission to make a lavish edition of *The Divine Comedy* for the nobleman Lorenzo di Pierfrancesco de' Medici.

Botticelli manages to represent much of Dante's narrative with just one panoptic image, filling his map with an astounding amount of detail and motifs, with some of the figures featured measuring just ½in (1cm) tall. (The map itself measures just 19in/47.5cm wide.) With the master artist's elegant meticulousness, most of Dante's story can be 'read' in the image, and reflects both Botticelli's lifelong passion for, and expert knowledge of, the fourteenth-century poem.

The obsession with Dantean cartography largely subsided after the sixteenth century, but a resurgence of interest in the

ABOVE AND OPPOSITE LEFT: *Maps of hell and,* OPPOSITE RIGHT: *an overview of the universe of the Divine Comedy, by Michelangelo Caetani, Duke of Sermoneta, 1855.*

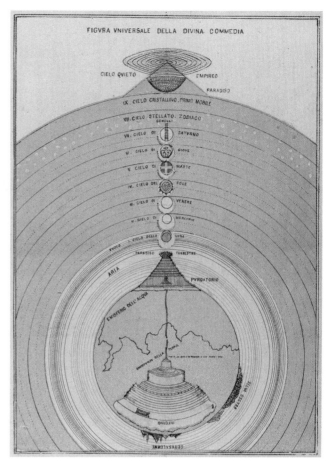

nineteenth century was most notably headed by Michelangelo Caetani, Duke of Sermoneta and a cosmopolitan scholar. Over three hundred years after Manetti in 1855, Caetani published a series of Dantean topographic maps under the title *La materia della Divina commedia di Dante Alighieri dichiarata in VI tavole* (The Content of Dante's *Divine Comedy* Described in Six Plates), presenting a more modern geographical envisioning using early chromolithography, printed by the monks at Monte Cassino. Maintaining the considered scientific of the infernal cartographic tradition, Caetani's maps reflect the enduring appeal of Dante's poetry, hypnotic to artist, writer and scientist alike through the centuries. 'Dante and Shakespeare divide the world between them,' wrote T. S. Elliot. 'There is no third.'

FOLLOWING PAGES: *Botticelli's* Map of Hell, *inspired by Dante.*

THE EVOLUTION OF HELL

The wealth of ornate detail that rendered the Dantean cosmos so alluring to cartographic attempts would dominate the popular image of the afterlife in the sixteenth century, capping the tradition of the hell tours of medieval mystics with Dante's dazzling artistic triumph of early Renaissance literature. But by the early seventeenth century, in Protestant England especially, there was little interest in the precise mapping of hell, nor the gradation of sins established by Dante. One either joined God in heaven, or not. Separation from His presence was the punishment, and so elaborate hierarchies of specific tortures at the hands of demons were deemed pointless. Catholic hellfire preachers, on the other hand, balanced the punishment of spiritual deprivation with the physical horrors to full effect.

The Bavarian Jesuit Jeremias Drexel (1581-1638) was known for hammering home the terrors with imaginative eloquence. A typical snippet from his *Considerations…* (1632) is: 'Their Torments shall continue many Millions of Years without one sweet or refreshing Moment… They shall gnash their teeth with cold, and the Fire shall force them to lament and weep… If the Gout or Stone is in one short Night… severely painful and grievous to us, consider we with ourselves how shall we endure to lie in the Flames Night and Day for Thousands of Years.'

While listing the torments of hell (inner and outer darkness, weeping, hunger, intolerable stench, fire) – specifically while detailing the stench of flatulence from the multitude, and all the smells from the 'World Sewer' – Drexel performs a curious calculation. There are one hundred thousand million of the damned tightly pressed together in hell, he writes, all having to fit into the area size of 1 sq. mile (2.5 sq. km):

'They will be penned like dogs or pigs, or like grapes in a winepress, like pickled tuna in a barrel, like bricks in the furnace of a lime-kiln, like a ewe-lamb on the spit, like plumbs being flambed, like sheep having their throats cut in the market.'

The Jesuit preacher Louis Bourdaloue (1632-1704), whose sermons went on for so long that female members of his congregation would bring chamber pots with them to hide under their dresses (which they called 'bourdaloues'), dismissed the idea of torturous demons in hell. Instead, the sinner would be tormented by his own past crimes: 'Those abominable impurities, those enormous injustices, those profanations of holy things, those signs of contempt toward

ABOVE: *An angel leading a soul into hell, in an oil painting by a follower of Hieronymus Bosch.*

OPPOSITE: *The Last Judgement panel of the Early Netherlandish artist Jan van Eyck's* Crucifixion and Last Judgement *diptych, c.1430-1440. The mid-fifteenth-century painting is unusual in that it bridges both the traditional concept of hell and the new fashion for personifying a skeletal Death.*

The Last Judgement *triptych by the Flemish painter Hans Memling, painted between 1467 and 1471. The right-hand panel shows the damned being dragged to hell.*

God… these are the monsters that infest the reprobate, who encompass him around, who seize him with the most lively terrors.' (Bourdaloue, *On Hell*, page 552.)

This was also the Age of Enlightenment, and while there was a new interest in overthrowing dogmatic religious authority, for some there was an adoption of a rigid literalism about hell with an Enlightenment interest in examining how it might be explained in natural terms. What was the composition of hellfire? Where on the globe could hell be located? Or, for that matter, where in the universe? Embodying Enlightenment empiricism was Tobias Swinden (1659-1719), who in his *Enquiry Into the Nature and Place of Hell* attempted to account for scriptural assertions with geological science.

Swinden's investigation led him to make the original suggestion that hell could not in fact be within the Earth, for several reasons. For a start, there was not enough fuel within the planet to sustain the eternal infernal fires. It was also clearly too small an area to hold every fallen angel – for it was traditionally known that their number was comparable to a third of the stars in the heavens – as well as every condemned soul from the entirety of man's history, even when one allows for the reported overcrowding. (Swinden scoffed at Drexel's

One of the most vivid illustrations of how souls are set upon by the demons of hell, by Luca Signorelli (1441-1523).

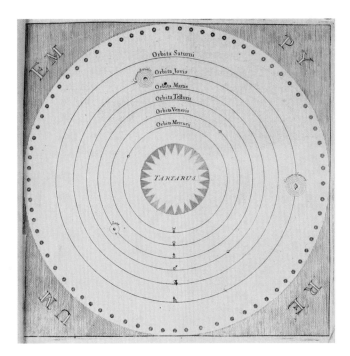

The second plate from Tobias Swinden's An Enquiry Into the Nature and Place of Hell *(1714), in which the author maps his theory of the hellish Tartarus being at the centre of the Sun.*

German 'mile' calculation.) But the clincher for Swinden was that the Earth was incapable of generating the temperatures necessary for the fires of hell – how could it, when covered with so much cooling water?

Swinden's solution to these problems was ingenious in its simplicity: hell must be in the Sun. There was clearly enough fuel there to sustain perpetual fire of sufficient soul-scorching heat. 'If anyone be so stupid as to doubt, or hardy to deny this, let him only betake himself to those parts of the world that lie directly under the Line [the equator], and there expose his naked body to its scorching beams, when in its full meridian strength.' With a size over a million times that of the Earth, there was also plenty of room in the Sun to contain hell's population. The dark spots that astronomers sighted on the Sun's surface? Those were glimpses of the darkness in which the souls were imprisoned. And so it was settled, wrote Swinden, that our star was indisputably 'Tartarus or local hell'.

The Tuscan missionary Giovanni Pinamonti produced his own measured hell in 1693 in *Hell Opened to Christians*, which centuries later would give James Joyce much inspiration for his *Portrait of the Artist as a Young Man* (1916). In it he writes that the walls of hell are 4000 miles (6450km) thick. The damned are so tightly packed within that they're unable to

move, and too weak to fend off the worms gnawing at their eyes. 'Every one that is damned will be like a lighted furnace, which has its own flames in itself; all that filthy blood will boil in the veins, the brains in the skull, the heart in the breast, the bowels within the unfortunate body, surrounded with an abyss of fire.'

Meanwhile, artistic visions of hell followed the Protestant idea of separation from God being the worst punishment, while also drawing inspiration from contemporary literature

as much as the lamentations of the preacher's pulpit. With *Paradise Lost* (1667), John Milton intended his work to 'justify the ways of God to man', but it provoked curious fascination with a captivating portrayal of Satan, and it is through following Satan, and his every turn of his thinking, that we enter and explore hell, in a story that focuses on freedom of will over the traditional teachings of predestination.

After a brutal war with the archangel Michael and his angelic army, Satan and his troops are: 'Hurl'd headlong flaming from th' Ethereal Sky / With hideous ruin and combustion down / To bottomless perdition, there to dwell / In Adamantine chains and penal Fire.' For nine days they tumble through Chaos, until: 'Hell at last / Yawning receiv'd them whole, and on them clos'd, / Hell their fit habitation fraught with fire / Unquenchable, the house of woe and pain.' They crash into a burning lake, and on emerging from the sulphurous flames discover they have lost both their angelic form and their heavenly surroundings, instead finding: ' A Dungeon horrible, on all sides round / As one great

Mankind's Eternal Dilemma – The Choice Between Virtue and Vice, by Frans Francken the Younger, 1633.

LEFT: A Scheme of the Solar System with the Orbits of the Planets and Comets belonging thereto…*(1712) by William Whiston (1667-1752). The English theologian believed comets are populated 'hells for tormenting the damned with perpetual vicissitudes of heat and cold'.*

BELOW: Satan Rousing the Rebel Angels*, engraved by Michael Burgesse, from the 1688 Tonson edition of John Milton's* Paradise Lost *(first published 1667).*

Furnace flam'd, yet from those flames / No light, but rather darkness visible / Serv'd only to discover sights of woe.' This last sentence in particular has been the subject of much discussion over the centuries – the oxymoronic 'darkness visible', an antithesis of the light of heaven, conveys in just two words a chillingly powerful sense of the symbolic gloom of hell, as a pure void of all goodness through the absence of God.

Milton then presents a second image of hell, as the demons construct a capital for themselves, Pandemonium, exalting Satan with a palace and a throne, in imitation of God. The demons sing and hold raucous debates, and hell operates as an ironic mirror of heaven and its angelic organisation, until Milton reveals the true sorrow of hell with the third form – the inner, psychological hell. This burns at the core of the tragedy of Satan, as he laments in a soliloquy at the beginning of Book IV: 'Which way I fly is Hell; myself am Hell.' This is ultimately the truest hell of Milton's universe, the spiritual state, the hell one carries within oneself, inescapable, more terrible than imprisonment in any location.

TORMENTO DA ETERNIDADE

This is not to say that reported expeditions to hell were now purely confined to fictional literature. In 1745, the Swedish theologian and mystic Emanuel Swedenborg was dining in a London tavern when the lights suddenly went out. A figure appeared in the corner of the room, and shouted to him: 'Do not eat too much!' Swedenborg ran away in fright, but later that night the figure reappeared to him in his dreams, introduced himself as the Lord, and said that He had chosen Swedenborg to reveal the true meaning of the Bible for Swedenborg to share with the world.

He went on to publish the accounts of a series of visions and tours of the afterlife, including *Concerning the Earths in Our Solar System*, in which he reports humanoid life on the Moon, Venus and Mars; but the most famous work is *Heaven and Hell* (1758), in which he travels down to hell in a brass elevator. His accounts are at once strikingly similar, yet also markedly different, to the hell-tour accounts of medieval saints. 'From Hell there continually exhales and descends the effort of doing evil', he writes, which is maintained in balance with the virtuous exhalations of heaven. There are, he reports, multiple hells to be found in a landscape similar in topography to that of Earth:

There are hells everywhere, both under the mountains, hills and rocks, and under the plains and valleys… All, when looked into, appear dark and dusky; but the infernal spirits who are within them wind themselves in a sort of light resembling that emitted from ignited charcoal. Their eyes are adapted to receive that light in consequence of their having been, while they lived in the world, in darkness with respect to divine truth… All [the apertures] are covered over except when evil spirits from the world of spirits are cast in…

Swedenborg also glimpsed the housing in a few of the lesser hell sectors, revealing a hellscape of recognisable urban deprivation and decay, with the surprising information of the existence of bordellos in hell:

In the milder hells are seen what appear like rude cottages, sometimes arranged contiguously as in a city with lanes and streets; and within these houses are infernal spirits who are engaged in continuous altercations, displays of enmity, beatings and efforts to tear one another to pieces; while in the streets and lanes are committed robberies and depredations. In some hells are brothels disgusting to behold, being full of all sorts of filth and excrement.

Opposite and Above:
Illustrations from Desenganno dos Peccadores *(Disillusion of Sinners) by the Jesuit priest Alexandre Perier, first published in Rome in 1724. Sense-based tortures that await sinners include demons hammering metal bolts through the eye, blasting hell's trumpets and force-feeding with scorpions, lizards and snakes.*

AY DENOS OTROS, PARA QUE PECAMOS YANO AY REMEDIO EN EL YNFIERNO ADONDE NO AY QUE BER ALGUN ORDEN, SINO ETERNAL CONFUSION.

AY DE MI QUE ARDIENDO QUEDO AY QUE PUDE YANO PUEDO AY QUE POH SIEMPRE HEDE ARDER AY QUE ADIOS NUNCA HEDE VER.

An 1802 mural depicting hell by Tadeo Escalante, at San Juan Bautista in Huaro, Peru.

His contemporaries were convinced that he would find no readership and be swiftly forgotten, but in fact Swedenborg's writings resonated long through the nineteenth century, finding footing with those averse to the science and reason of an Enlightened Age. Indeed, his work formed the basis of the Church of New Jerusalem, founded with the claim of 'completing' the other Christian doctrines.

In 1879, Pope Leo XIII issued a bull that affirmed the existence of an eternal hell and of the Devil; and in the minds of young Victorians the reality of hell was vividly reinforced by the best-selling book *The Sight of Hell*. This was written by the appropriately named Catholic priest John Furniss (1809-1865), who stands alone in the history of hell as the only writer to have published a treatise on the tortures of hell written specifically for 'children and young persons', in gruesome detail:

The little child is in the red-hot oven. Hear how it screams to come out; see how it turns and twists itself about in the fire. It beats its

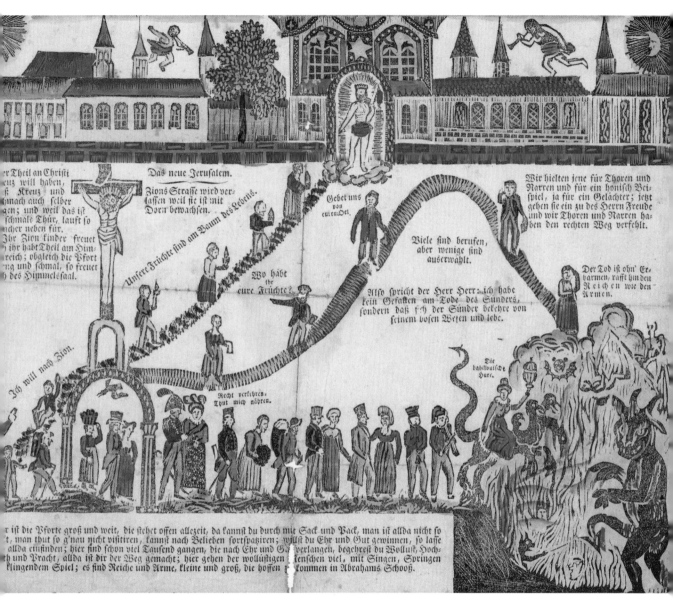

head against the roof of the oven. It stamps its little feet on the floor… God was very good to this little child. Very likely God saw it would get worse and worse and never repent, and so it would have been punished more severely in Hell. So God in his mercy called it out of the world in early childhood.'

A rare Amish allegorical broadside from c.1820, showing the paths to heaven and hell. At the top is the grand city of the 'New Jerusalem'; along the bottom, the rich walk into the fires of perdition.

Though the image of hell in the popular consciousness has since remained the same, fed by these narrative and artistic traditions, the various infernal notions that have so inspired these authors and artists of course continue to maintain a

The Roads to Heaven and Hell.
Die Wege zum Himmel und zur Hölle.

... Come unto me all ye that labour and are heavy laden, and I will give you rest.   Mat. 11, 28. ...

Kommt alle her zu mir, die ihr mühselig und beladen seid,   ich will euch erquicken.   Matth. 11, 28.

hold over popular imaginations. Even today, every so often an eccentric contribution to the tradition of the saintly vision and tour of hell will pop up – we need only look at the commercial success of a recent trend of modern hell visits, with books like *23 Minutes in Hell* (2006) to find this in evidence. 'I wasn't yet aware of it', begins the American author Bill Wiese, 'but I had fallen into hell.'

On an otherwise unremarkable Sunday night, on 22 November 1998, the southern California estate agent was in bed with his wife when suddenly 'without any notice, I found myself being hurled through the air… I landed in what appeared to be a prison cell. I was completely naked… This was not a dream.' Wiese details his encounter with two odorous beasts of evil who spoke in a blasphemous language, and then a meeting with Jesus, who told him to share his story. Then he awoke screaming on his living room floor.

Both Christian and secular critics came together in scepticism. On Wiese's description of hell being so hot that it was 'far beyond any possibility of sustaining life', Rob Moll of *Christianity Today* points out that, you know, it being hell this wasn't so much of a problem. John Sutherland, writing about the book in the *New Statesman*, also took issue with Wiese's writing, especially his description of the sound of billions of tortured souls screaming in infinite agony as 'annoying'. Naturally, the book sold well regardless, spending three weeks on the extended *New York Times* best-seller list for paperback non-fiction, despite the criticism and Wiese's oblivious statement that his book ' will be the closest you will ever come to experiencing hell for yourself'. As for why God would choose an estate agent to be thrown into hell for such a torturous episode – well, who are we to fathom His mysterious ways?

OPPOSITE: The Roads to Heaven and Hell, *1896.*

LIMBO, PURGA
AND OTHER

MIDWORLDS

While to the Western European it is limbo and purgatory that are best known, the notion of a post-Earth intermediate realm somewhere between heaven and hell can be found in belief systems around the world. The Zoroastrian idea of Hamistagan is one such example. Hamistagan (in equilibrium or stationary) is a neutral place reserved for the souls of those who are classed as neither good nor evil, where they await Judgement Day as it is mentioned in the ninth-century Zoroastrian text *Dādestān i Denig* (Religious Decisions) by the high priest Manushchihr.

As we will see, Hamistagan is more akin to the Catholic idea of limbo than the idea of purgatory, as it is thought of as a dull waiting room rather than an arena of punishment and purification by fire. Here, relates Manushchihr, the departed can relive their lives in the attempt to perform more good deeds in a realm not unlike our own, so as to eventually elevate themselves to the paradise of the House of Song. While existence in this place was originally described as an insensate experience, later texts describe the temperatures as similar to Earth, cold in winter and warm in summer.

In Islam, a comparable place is Barzakh (obstacle, hindrance or partition), a temporary state that exists following death and before the day of resurrection. Here, sinners are punished while the sufficiently virtuous enjoy comforts. (Children however, being innocent, are given exemption and pass straight to heaven, to the love of Abraham.) Barzakh is mentioned only three times in the Qur'an, and only once specifically as a border between the terrestrial and celestial (the other two instances are metaphorically as an isthmus between saltwater – i.e. this world – and the sweet fresh water of the next), and so it has been weighed with varying importance among Muslim scholars, with some ignoring it entirely.

The medieval Islamic jurist Ibn al-Qayyim (AD 1292-1350) developed the idea and wrote that souls that congregate in Barzakh are grouped together with those of an equal level of purity. In Sufism, the Arab Andalusian Muslim scholar Ibn Arabi (1165-1240) places great importance on Barzakh, declaring it not just a borderland but also a crucial bridge between the Corporeal World and the Spiritual World, and states that without it neither would exist.

In the reincarnation cycle of Buddhism, the term *bardo* came into use following the death of the Buddha, to refer to an intermediate stage between death and rebirth that is often compared to the idea of limbo. It is particularly important in Tibetan Buddhism, where it is a focus of the text *Bardo Thodol* (Liberation Through Hearing During the Intermediate State), better known in the West as the *Tibetan Book of the Dead*. According to tradition, this text was composed in the eighth century by Padmasambhava, considered the Second Buddha by the Nyingma school, the oldest Buddhist school in Tibet.

OPPOSITE AND RIGHT: *Persian chainmail shirt made of protective prayers, c.1500-1600. Each link is stamped on the obverse with the names of Allah and five leading imams of the Shi'a (i.e. Muhammad, Ali, Fatima, Hasan and Husayn), who are also known as* Panjtan (The Five) *or the* Ahl al-Kisa (People of the Cloak).

The work offers instructions on spotting the signs of death and which rituals to perform in the event, but most of its lessons are intended to be read not to the deceased, as is commonly thought, but by the living to visualise the afterlife, as a guide to navigating the intermediate world the dead experience following death for forty-nine days before the next rebirth.

The *Bardo Thodol* breaks down this intermediate form of existence into three states. In the immediate *chikhai bardo* (bardo of the moment of death), the deceased will experience the 'clear light of reality', or as close to it as one is able to reach; then comes the *chonyid bardo* (bardo of the experiencing of reality), in which one will catch glimpses of various forms of the Buddha; and then the *sidpa bardo* (bardo of rebirth), in which one experiences hallucinations ranging from hellish creatures to couples passionately entwined, depending on one's karmic level. Together with three other sections of the *bardo* – the state of waking consciousness; the state of *dhyana* (meditation); and the dream state during normal sleep – the categorisation of these six bardos serves as a map of the different broad states of consciousness.

In Western Europe, before the development of limbo and purgatory, the midworld most prominent in classical thought is that of Greek mythology – the part of Hades named the Asphodel Fields, or Asphodel Meadows, mentioned by Homer in the *Odyssey*. This was the destination of the dead who have not sufficient virtue to earn passage to the Elysian Fields, nor sufficient sin to be doomed to suffer in Tartarus, the most hellish part of Hades.

Homer's Asphodel Meadow, the place 'where the spirits of the dead dwell' (*Odyssey* 24:14), was traditionally thought of as a pleasant place by ancient Greek poets and commentators, who interpreted the word 'asphodel' (a kind of flower) to indicate it was a land of verdancy and a near paradise-like pleasance. So too did poets of post-Renaissance England like Alexander Pope (1688-1744), who makes reference to 'happy souls who dwell in yellow meads of asphodel'. In fact, the Asphodel Meadows described by Homer in three separate passages (*Odyssey* 11:539; 11:573; 24:13) are considerably grimmer. It is a true realm of Hades: mirthless, and so sunless as to be thick with inky darkness, where pale spirits of the dead scream and wail and wander aimlessly, with as much substance as shadows or dreams.

OPPOSITE: *Peaceful and wrathful deities of the* Bardo *in an eighteenth-century Tibetan painting.*

LIMBO

In Roman Catholic theology, there is the idea of limbo (from the Latin *limbus* – boundary), a state or location somewhere on the edge of hell. Nowhere in the Christian scriptures is limbo actually referenced, nor is it mentioned in the Catechism of the Catholic Church, the summary of Catholic beliefs commissioned by Pope John Paul in 1992. Rather, it is an idea that grew out of scriptural interpretation and extrapolative thinking in Europe in the Middle Ages, as a destination for those who died tainted with original sin, for whom joyful existence in God's company must therefore be withheld, but for whom banishment to eternal suffering in hell would also be counter to the nature of a benevolent God.

In fact, there are actually two separate limbo regions, necessary subdivisions that emerged from this reasoning – the *limbus infantum* (Limbo of the Infants) and the *limbus partum* (Limbo of the Patriarchs). The Limbo of the Infants was drawn from the few biblical references to Hades and Sheol to accommodate the souls of those children who die before their baptism, with their original sin intact but too young to have committed sinful actions. Clearly, a just God would not banish such unfortunates to eternal torment, and so a separate place must exist. 'Such infants as quit the body without being baptised', postulated the highly influential St Augustine, 'will be involved in the mildest condemnation of all.'

Many of St Augustine's fellow Latin Fathers (the authoritative group of thinkers and writers who contributed to and shaped the doctrines of Christianity in the Early Middle Ages), such as St Jerome (*c.*347-420), Avitus of Vienne (*c.*470-517/519) and Pope Gregory I (*c.*540-604) also shared this belief in limbo. The existence of infant souls in this place, it was hoped, is merely a temporary home for the young innocents, who will eventually progress to the care of heaven.

The Limbo of the Patriarchs, on the other hand, is the medieval name for a place wandered by those viewed favourably by God, regardless of sins committed, who must wait to be redeemed by Jesus Christ before they're granted entry to heaven. This limbo is another designated section of the Old Testament underworld of Hades, where all patriarchal

figures of the scriptures reside until freed by Christ's descent into hell following his death on the cross, an episode known as the Harrowing of Hell, for Christ's redemption is the only course to heaven – 'I am the way and the truth and the life,' he states in John 14:6. 'No one comes to the Father except through me.' This is the 'heaven's waiting room' limbo of modern popular consciousness, drawn from just a few references from gospels such as that of Luke, in which Jesus tells a parable of the rich man and the beggar named Lazarus, in which the latter is taken to heaven and the former is distraught to find himself in hell (Luke 16:22-25).

Descent of Christ into Limbo *by Bartolomé Bermejo (1440-1500), one of four altarpiece compartments.*

Christin Limbo, c.*1575, by a*
follower of Hieronymus Bosch.

From the 1st century AD, Christian writers interpreted this 'bosom of Abraham' as being the temporary place for souls awaiting their initiation into heaven, an interpretation followed by the Roman Catholic Church and the Eastern Orthodox Church (though, again, there is no use of the word 'limbo'). It was only fair that there should be a place of waiting for those who died before the time of Christ, reasoned writers such as Clement of Alexandria (*c*.150-*c*.215): 'It is not right that these should be condemned without trial, and that those alone who lived after the coming (of Christ) should have the advantage of the divine righteousness.'

In his *Inferno*, Dante maps limbo as the first circle of hell, though very different to the others, without the violent and frightful scenes of the ensuing layers. Here resides Dante's afterworld guide, Virgil, in a beautiful and bright castle surrounded by seven high walls and a moat and overlooking an 'emerald green' meadow of fresh grass. This he shares with other virtuous pre-Christian figures of antiquity including Hector, Julius Caesar, Virgil, Electra and Orpheus, and the Muslims Saladin and Averroes. Dante's limbo is a gloomy,

LEFT: *One of Gustave Doré's illustrations for Dante's* Inferno. *Plate XI: Canto IV: The Virtuous Pagans: 'Lost are we and only so far punished, / That without hope we live on in desire.'*

wooded plain, 'dark and deep and foggy', with a valley filled with what he initially takes to be cries of anguish but which he then realises are deeply sorrowful sighs of 'crowds, multitudinous and vast, of babies and of women and of men'. The sadness of the place soaks into him: 'Deep sorrow crushed my heart when I heard him, because both men and women of great worth I knew to be suspended here in limbo.'

As usual, it is Dante that gives us the most vivid image of the concept, although in modern Catholic theological thinking it is an idea all but disregarded. In 2007, the International Theological Commission, an advisory body to the Vatican, completed a three-year examination of the question of traditional limbo, and declared it an 'unduly restrictive view of salvation'.

BELOW: Christ's Descent into Limbo, *1470-1475, by Andrea Mantegna (1431-1506).*

PURGATORY

When visiting Italy, of all the sites that should be on the itinerary of those interested in the material traces of, and tributes to, the afterlife, the smallest is also perhaps the strangest. Churches that were established specifically for prayers for the souls of purgatory are relatively common. The church of Santa Maria delle Anime del Purgatorio ad Arco in central Naples, for example, dates back to 1638. When the Black Death tore through the populace in 1656, its vaults were crammed with the bodies of the dead – without proper burial, they were assumed to have been consigned to an eternity in purgatory. The church still hosts regular ceremonies of prayerful worship for those poor souls.

The Museo delle Anime del Purgatorio (Museum of the Souls of Purgatory) in Rome, on the other hand, is unique. This tiny 'museum', tucked into the vestry of the Chiesa del Sacro Cuore del Suffragio, offers the post-mortem-obsessed pilgrim the opportunity to see objects that were apparently physically touched, and scorched, by the burning souls of purgatory. After a chapel of the Chiesa del Sacro Cuore del Suffragio was damaged by a blaze, a priest named Victor Jou't noticed the scorched image of a human face on a wall. Deducing this to be the face of a purgatorial soul attempting to warn the living and appeal for prayers to help convey their souls to heaven, Jou't founded the museum. (Only a cynic would make a connection between this enterprise and the stack of bills to repair the church.) The museum hosts an array

The Museo delle Anime del Purgatorio, Rome, houses scorched artefacts that are claimed to have been touched by the burning souls of purgatory.

A map of an earthly entrance to purgatory on St Patrick's Island, by Wenceslaus Hollar, 1654.

of similarly scorched objects that Jou't subsequently collected together, including the burnt imprint of three fingers left in 1871 on the prayer book of Maria Zaganti by the deceased Palmira Rastelli, and a similar impression left on a book belonging to Marguerite Demmerlé of the Parish of Ellinghen, left by her mother-in-law in 1815, thirty years after she died.

The human need to believe in a just and merciful cosmos is a universal concern in many religious and cultural traditions – in Christianity (predominantly Catholicism), it was specifically answered with the conception of purgatory. Surely, it was thought, there must be a 'third place' where the average person – neither a habitual sinner nor a flawless saint – could go to be cleansed of minor sins that should not dictate an infernal sentence. In this place they would make peace with and earn forgiveness for any and all of these bad actions, be assuaged of guilt, and finally in newly purified and polished form qualify for entry to the perfection of heaven. Unlike the Jewish underworld Sheol, in the flame-filled intermediary world of purgatory the dead are subjected to torturous trials, most commonly of fire and ice (for purification, not punishment like those of hell), that could be eased and shortened by the living

with the offering of prayers – even *before* one's death – as a way
of earning good graces.

Though the formation of the idea of purifying fire has its
roots in Judeo-Christian antiquity, the authoritative afterlife
historian Jacques Le Goff has shown that the notion of purgatory
being an actual place only came into existence in Western Europe
much later, near the end of the twelfth century, and took firm
hold in the following century. It is not mentioned in the Bible,
which is the principal factor in the disagreement among
Christians as to whether such a state exists. Protestantism, for
example, has always denied the possibility, but the Catholic
Church continues to hold that 'all who die in God's grace and
friendship but still imperfectly purified' undergo the process
of purification of purgatory 'so as to achieve the holiness
necessary to enter the joy of heaven'. The practice of praying
for, and making offerings to, the dead has been in use ever
since the Church began, and is mentioned in 2 Maccabees
12:41-46, in which Judas Maccabeus sent money to Jerusalem to
arrange sacrifices in the temple for his soldiers killed in battle.

Compared to the remoteness of heaven, purgatory offered
to the living faithful an appealing form of contact with the

Holy Allegory *by Giovanni
Bellini, an enigmatic painting of
the sixteenth century, interpreted
as a depiction of purgatory.*

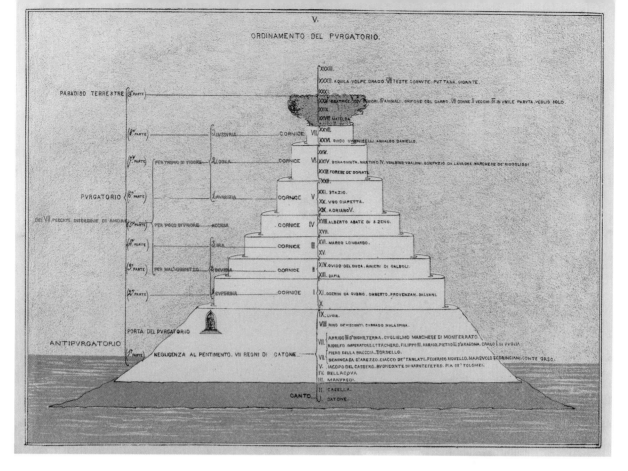

Michelangelo Caetani's map
The Ordering of Purgatory,
*based on Dante's descriptions,
published 1855.*

dead, and the hope that a sentence in hell could be avoided.
'Purgatory surpasses heaven and hell in poetry, because it
represents a future and the others do not', wrote François-René
de Chateaubriand (1768-1848). However, until the end of the
twelfth century, exactly *where* these souls were to reside and
these trials take place was not yet specified.

St Augustine was never fully convinced of the need of such
a cleansing process, but in his *City of God*, 21:26, reluctantly
concedes its existence. Robert Pullen (*c.*1080–*c.*1146), a cardinal
who went on to be chancellor of the Roman Catholic Church
in 1145, establishes first in his text *Sententiae* that *infernus…
locus est* (hell is a place), but displays puzzlement at where the
painful *ignis purgatorias* (purgatorial flames) should exist: 'Is it
in Heaven? Is it in Hell? Heaven does not seem appropriate to
tribulation, but torture does not seem appropriate to correction,
particularly not in our time… Where are those who are supposed
to do penance after death? In purgatorial places. Where are
those places? I do not yet know…'

William of Auvergne (1180-1249), bishop of Paris from 1228
until his death, makes the point in a treatise in his enormous
work *Magisterium divinale sive saientale* that there needs to be a

place of purgation (which he describes as 'an obvious fact') because of those who died suddenly – for example 'by the sword, suffocation or excess suffering' without having the time to complete their penance. He also remarks that all sins are not equal – the punishment for sins of murder and plunder should be different for those otherwise pure souls freighted with lesser sins, like excessive laughter or over-indulgence in food and drink; and for this expiation of such small sins a place is needed before they enter paradise. Not only does purgatory doubtlessly exist, but because of how common these lesser sins are, he suggests purgatory is heavily populated, at the expense of hell. William also sets about rationalising the fire of purgatory, describing how fire comes in varieties: in Sicily, for example, it is said that one type turns hair phosphorescent without burning it. And then there are fireproof animals like the salamander, for instance. Therefore, might not God have created a special kind of mild fire to get rid of slight and incompletely expiated sins?

Pope Gregory I suggested in his anecdotes that the purging process takes place where the sin was originally committed. Other authors were torn between placing it below the earth, in the upper regions of hell, or locating it, as Bede did, on a mountain, closer to heaven. Most agreed though that some sort of fire, different to that of Gehenna, was involved.

Regardless, the doctrine of purgatory had a terrific, transformative impact on late medieval Christianity, inspiring many great works of ecclesiastical architecture, as the wealthy were keen to donate large amounts for repeated, even perpetual, masses to be held for them, in which the suffrages of the congregation would grease their souls' transition through the purgatorial process to paradise.

In England, one Oxford College, All Souls, was specifically established with the purpose of praying for the souls of English soldiers who were killed on the field of the Battle of Agincourt in 1415. As Jacques Le Goff puts it in *The Birth of Purgatory*: 'For the Church, what a marvellous instrument of power! Purgatory brought to the Church not only new spiritual power but also, to put it bluntly, considerable profit... Much of this profit went to the mendicant orders, ardent propagandists of the new doctrine. And finally, the "infernal" system of indulgences found powerful support in the idea of Purgatory.'

In sixteenth-century England, among the bitter arguments between Catholics and Protestants was the latter's severe

Mount Purgatory from Ugo Foscolo's La Commedia di Dante Alighieri, *1825.*

reproaching of the former for belief in purgatory, the 'invented world' not mentioned in the Bible. This polemic dispute was often sharply focused on what became a traditional site of Catholic pilgrimage, St Patrick's Purgatory, an island in the Lough Derg in County Donegal, Ireland. Legend told that St Patrick mistook a salmon in the River Derg for a stepping stone and rode it across to the island, where he fasted for the entirety of Lent. Subsequently, he was given the power to bring seven souls out of hell every Saturday from a cave. Thus it was believed that this was an earthly entrance to purgatory, and so in the twelfth century began the tradition of pilgrims travelling to the island and being shut up in the cave, emerging in the morning to tell terrifying visions of punishments, fires and demons.

Detail of a miniature of Dante and Virgil with Pope Adrian V, Hugh Capet and Statius, in purgatory; below: Dante and Virgil at the gates of purgatory. From a manuscript dated between 1444 and 1450.

Purgatory, from the Très Riches Heures du Duc de Berry *manuscript by Jean Colombe, 1412-1416. Tormented souls await purification, when angels will carry them to paradise.*

Attempts were made by Elizabethan and later governments to close down the site of worship, but these were always thwarted. St Patrick's Purgatory is mentioned in texts from as early as 1185, and cartographically is significant in that it is featured on European maps from as early as the fifteenth century, and is the only Irish feature marked on Martin Behaim's world map of 1492. Wenceslaus Hollar produced a dedicated map of the island in 1654, marking the various stations or 'prayer stops' of its pilgrims – hence why the island is known locally as Station Island.

As with hell, the features of purgatory coalesced and solidified with the poetic genius of Dante, just over one

hundred years after its conception, ensuring its endurance in popular memory. Dante harmonised the fragments of details in *Purgatorio* (Purgatory), the second part of his *Divine Comedy*: 'the noblest representation of Purgatory ever conceived by the mind of man', writes Le Goff. In an allegory of the penitent Christian life, Dante climbs up the Mount of Purgatory, the only land to be found in the Southern Hemisphere, still under the guidance of the Roman poet Virgil (until Beatrice takes over in the last four cantos). Both hell and the Mount were created by the impact of Satan falling from heaven, reports Dante as he ascends, traversing seven tiers (linked with the seven deadly sins) of ordeals and suffering, until finally reaching the Earthly Paradise at the summit at noon on Wednesday, 30 March (or 13 April, with the Gregorian calendar adjustment).

Today, the Church of England continues to deny 'the Romish Doctrine concerning Purgatory', while the Eastern Orthodox Church, Oriental Orthodox Churches and parts of Anglican, Lutheran and Methodist traditions allow for there to be some form of purification after death and prayer for the deceased. Purgatory is still a part of Catholic Church thought, though popes John Paul II and Benedict XVI both clarified that the term 'purgatory' is not an actual place, but a state of being, and church dogma holds no mention of any location nor specific purifying process – these details are left to individual opinion.

William Blake, Beatrice addressing Dante *at the summit of Mount Purgatory, site of the Earthly Paradise, or Garden of Eden, in an illustration of Canto 29 of Dante's* Purgatorio. *Beatrice is borne by the 'chariot triumphal', drawn by a griffin.*

HEAVENS, PARADISES

Hoping for the reward of a post-death world of peace and pleasure is as primal as the heat of hell; but the place to find it – heaven, paradise, utopia – usually has more nebulous, elusive geography than its infernal antipode. To find the latter, usually one has only to look down. Hells and underworlds have an earthly geology and animality to them – volcanoes hint at the fire contained beneath the Earth's surface, caves offer tantalising doorways. Heavens and paradises possess more of an 'elsewhereness', a vagueness of perfection, their detail blasted away by dazzling light, existing before, after or beyond time, somewhere in distant exotic kingdoms or islands across the oceans, or beyond the impenetrable, unclimbable, sky.

And yet, paradoxically, just as their specifics are unknowable, heavens are similar to hells in the way they are mirrors of contemporary societies. The skilled hunters of the Native American A'aninin people of Montana historically believed in the afterlife of the Big Sand, where their spirits could continue to hunt and feed on the spirits of animals, to their hearts' content. For the Admiralty Islanders on Manus (near New Guinea), life continues after death in pretty much identical fashion. Your property remains your own, as does your profession. Reo F. Fortune writes in *Manus Religion* (1935) that if the deceased had been a policeman he remains a policeman in the afterlife, collecting taxes paid by his fellow ghosts. The dead of the Ngaju Dayak (South Kalimantan, Borneo) go to Lewu Liau, a 'neighbouring' village set in fertile country, with a river teeming with fish and woods filled with game.

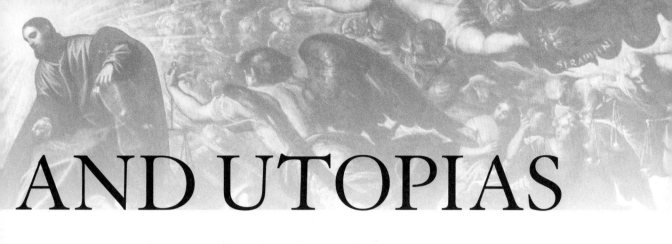

AND UTOPIAS

In Christianity, the bureaucracy and municipality of the afterlife became more of a prevalent theme as the urbanisation of medieval Europe flourished, and the construction of great cathedrals brought to earth the towering archaeology of the heavenly City of God, the New Jerusalem, promised in the Bible to be brought to the earthly plane by God as part of Judgement Day at the end of time. First, though, we begin with the agricultural ancient Egyptians, who dreamt of gaining eternal life in the fruitful *A'aru*, the Fields of Rushes.

The central detail of Tintoretto's enormous Il Paradiso *at the Doge's Palace, Venice, painted after 1588.*

A'ARU OF ANCIENT EGYPT

Originally, the heavenly afterlife of the ancient Egyptians was reserved for just one man: the pharaoh. The oldest Egyptian funerary texts, the *Pyramid Texts* of *c.*2400-2300 BC, were written solely for royal use. Following death, the pharaoh climbs the sky: 'You shall bathe in the starry firmament… the sun-folk shall call out to you, for the Imperishable Stars have raised you aloft.' They then join the night as a star: 'You will regularly ascend with Orion from the eastern region of the sky, and you will regularly descend with Orion into the western region of the sky.' They will then take their place with the sun god himself, and eventually surpass even the gods by hunting and eating them: 'The King has appeared again in the sky, he is crowned as the Lord of the Horizon; he has broken the back-bones and

A painting in the tomb of the ancient Egyptian artisan Sennedjem (c.1295-1213 BC), at Deir el-Medina on the west bank of the Nile, showing Sennedjem and his wife Iineferti working happily in the Fields of Rushes.

has taken the hearts of the gods… He has swallowed the intelligence of every god.' (*Pyramid Texts*, Utterances 273-274.)

In the later *Coffin Texts*, and the later-still *Book of the Dead*, the afterlife was gradually opened to all. When exploring the infernal aspects of the *Duat* or Other World (see page 20), the deceased ancient Egyptian had to first embark on a torturous journey through the underworld. The hellscape of fire and demonic ambuscades ultimately gives way to the Hall of Ma'at, gateway to the final destination of paradise – assuming one passes the judgement of Anubis, who weighs one's heart to measure virtue. If found wanting, the dead are devoured into non-existence by the crocodilian god Ammit; but if one is found to have lived virtuously, having recited the right prayers and made all confessions correctly, then entrance is granted to the fields of A'aru (sometimes 'Earu'), the Fields of Rushes, the perfect land of Osiris.

This was the paradise of the ancient Egyptian afterlife for all virtuous Egyptians, its lush, watered, green fields the very antipode of daily Egyptian life. Pictured as a series of islands covered in endless fields of rushes, A'aru was thought to be located somewhere in the east, from where the sun rose, its stretches of reeds being reminiscent of those that bordered the earthly Nile Delta. These are perfect grounds for ideal hunting and farming for food, sustaining the dead for eternity.

A'aru has in abundance many of the pleasures of the terrestrial realm – rich blue skies, boats for river cruises, drinking, fighting, marriage and the pantheon of gods and goddesses in residence for continued worship. The dead are designated their own plot of land among the fields with the responsibility to maintain it, but for those used to paying others to perform manual labour *the ushabti* figurines with which they were buried were equipped with agricultural tools to work the fields for their master, and after about 1000 BC these figurine workforces were even led by a *ushabti* foreman who carried a flail to flog the more lazy of the worker dolls.

A linen ball, found in Grave 518 at Tarkhan, Egypt. About 4500 years ago, loving parents placed this toy in the grave of their child to play with in the afterlife.

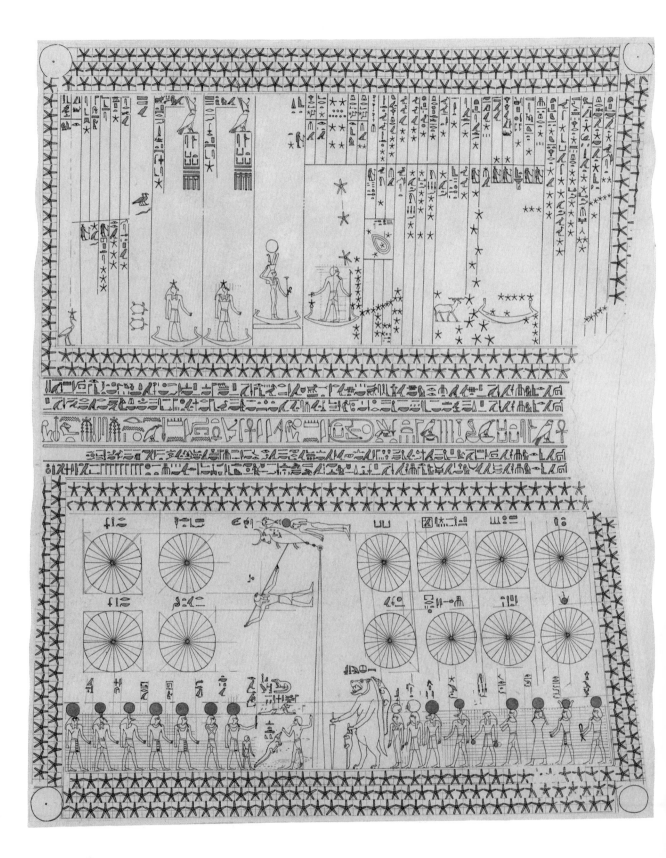

To be resurrected in this paradise was the point of every afterlife ritual, ceremony and incantation of Egyptian life, and of mummification – the body being preserved in order to best enjoy the blissful delights of A'aru. As the English Egyptologist Sir E. A. Wallis Budge quotes a rejoicing spirit in *Egyptian Religion* (1900): 'I have snared feathered fowl and fed upon the finest of them. I have seen Osiris, my father, and I have gazed upon my mother, and I have made love… I am led into celestial regions, and I make the things of earth to flourish; and there is joy of heart… I have tied up my boat in the celestial lakes… I have recited the prescribed words with my voice, and I have ascribed praises unto the gods.'

When it was just the pharaohs who were permitted entry, in texts the dead king is often described as climbing the sky in the form of a falcon, or goose; sometimes, he rides a grasshopper, or a cloud or a smoke-plume of incense; while in others he ascends a staircase or a ladder composed of beams of sunlight. It's thought that this is one reason behind the design of step-pyramids – the true pyramids that came later – erected over the tombs of the pharaohs, in representation of this sunbeam staircase notion. (It is a trademark contradiction of Egyptian belief, with its ideas developed over millennia, that the afterlife is thought of as both a kind of underworld and a high celestial realm.)

The social hierarchy and class division of terrestrial Egypt were carried over in the afterlife, with pharaohs keeping their deific status as gods. This, however, could be subject to sabotage by the living successor – when a pharaoh was succeeded by his rival, there is evidence of the latter defacing the tomb and monuments of the predecessor, to wreck his or her chances of reaching paradise. One theory suggests that the ancient desecration of Queen Hatshepsut was committed by her successor and stepson Thutmose III, for just this reason. Over the years, the exclusivity of the afterlife was gradually eased in traditional belief, although it was of course still the rich who could afford the practices of mummification and extravagant entombing that stood one the best chance of securing entry to the fields of A'aru.

OPPOSITE: *The celestial diagram adorning the ceiling of the tomb of the Egyptian architect Senenmut (fl. 1473), high steward to Queen Hatshepsut, showing the deities associated with the constellations.*

HEAVENS OF ANCIENT INDIA

Matching the dizzying variety of hells in Hinduism are its heavenly realms, also considered to be temporary stations in an ongoing journey of the soul through the great cycle of life, death and rebirth known as *samsara*. Ultimately, the goal of the good Hindu is not to reach a heaven comparable to the Christian idea, but to perform enough good deeds throughout one's multiple lives to finally achieve *moksha* (the release from the suffering of the material and bondage of *samsara*) to find a spiritual enlightenment and oneness with Brahman, the One Supreme Self.

Nevertheless, there is a complex structure to Hindu cosmology, which comprises multiple high realms. So what is the nature of the universe in which they sit? In the Hindu cosmos, Time is infinite – the universe enjoys a lifetime of one

A c.1810 illustration of the paradise of the Hindu god Shiva, believed to be at the summit of Mount Meru in Tibet. There can be found the god in sexual union with his beautiful consort, Parvati.

kalpa (day of Brahma), a period of 432 billion years, at the end of which time the universe is destroyed and Brahma creates a new one, in an endless cosmic cycle.

In terms of cosmic structure, both the *Brahmanda Purana* and the *Bhagavata Purana* texts describe a layered universe of fourteen *lokas* (esoteric planes), which are as much a category of being as they are a celestial region. The seven lower realms (Patalas) we have examined previously (see Hells of Ancient India, page 32); of the upper seven, the first is Bhu-loka (the earth plane); and then there are the six higher realms (Vyahrtis) which are, in descending order:

1. Satya-loka, the highest realm
2. Tapar-loka
3. Jana-loka
4. Mahar-loka
5. Svarga-loka (the paradise realm of the god Indra)
6. Bhuvar-loka, the Sun/Moon plane

The two of particular interest here are Svarga-loka, and the highest plane, Satya-loka. To locate Indra's plane of Svarga-loka, a group of heavenly worlds where the virtuous might find themselves reborn to enjoy its pleasures before their next

ABOVE: *An illustration of heaven from the seventeenth-century* Mewar Ramayana *(Rama's journey) – the finest surviving copy of the 2500-year-old story. Here Rama and his procession reach the banks of the River Sarayu, to enter the waters at bottom left and ascend to heaven.*

FOLLOWING PAGES: *Also from the* Mewar Ramayana, *a fantastic depiction of the giant Kumbhakarṇa, cursed by Brahma to a life spent asleep. The demon king Rāvaṇa sends an army of demon recruiters to try to wake the monster by making a great noise, striking him with weapons, screaming in his ear and playing musical instruments.*

incarnation, one must gaze up to the cloud-covered peaks of the towering Mount Meru, on which the heavenly realms balance. In Hinduism, the cosmic mountain is the highest point on Earth, centre of all creation and the rotations of the stars and planets, and home to Brahma. The holy five-peaked mountain enjoys this importance in Jain and Buddhist cosmology also, and its influence can be seen on the design of multitiered roofs of numerous significant temples across these religions. In Hindu tradition, the mountain, standing somewhere to the north of the Himalayas, is estimated to be 84,000 *yojanas* high, which works out to about 672,000 miles (1,100,000km) – 85 times the Earth's diameter.

Above the peak of this behemoth, sandwiched between other heavenly tiers, is Svarga-loka, housing righteous souls not yet pure enough to achieve the freedom of *moksha*. Svarga-loka's capital city is Amaravati, where Indra, king of the *devas* (an overall term for benevolent supernatural beings), rules from an enormous jewelled palace called Vaijayanta, which stretches across 800 miles (1300km) in circumference and rises 40 miles (64km) in height. Here one can wander the great celestial gardens of Nandana Vana, enjoying sacred trees like the Kalpavriksha, which grants wishes; and inhale the perfumes of hibiscuses, roses, hyacinths and honeysuckles while equally-as-sweet music plays gently in the background.

The numerous palaces are gold and smell of almonds;
their furniture is also made of gold, their pillars diamond,
all designed by Lord Vishwakarma, son of Lord Brahma and
architect of the gods. Music, dancing and festivities fill the days.
All of this enjoyment is dependent on having gained access via
the entrance guarded by Airavata, a formidable, divine, white
'elephant of the clouds', a fighting elephant with five trunks
and ten tusks, and the battle-steed of choice of Indra himself.

Far above this paradise realm of gold and elephants,
at a distance of many tens of millions of *yojanas*, is Satya-
loka (world of truth), the highest realm. This flower-filled
garden is home to Brahma, the creator god, and the goddess
Sarasvati and is the most blissful of celestial levels one can
hope to reach, although as with every other heavenly tier it
is an impermanent experience. Satya-loka is a vast garden of

enormous lotus flowers vibrant with divine power; and at the centre is the gigantic palace known as Brahmapura, the seat of Brahma. The lotus flower is closely associated with Brahma – some *Puranas* relate his origins as emerging from the flower, while connected to the navel of Lord Vishnu. Earlier texts suggest Brahma created himself, in a golden egg known as Hiranyagarbha, before generating the universe, the *Vedas* and the human race.

Hindu cosmology is a field of potentially endless exploration, with so many varieties of systems put forth over the centuries. This is partly due to the fact that each text of the *Puranas* literature must have a cosmology section, and these are often littered with as many questing, curiosity-driven ponderings as there are cosmic statements. New ideas were not instantly dismissed, but considered, adapted and absorbed; yet at the core remains the powerful idea of how the universe and the individual being are miscible. 'Because You are unlimited', writes the author of the *Bhagavata Purana* (10.87.41), 'neither the lords of heaven nor even You Yourself can ever reach the end of Your glories. The countless universes, each enveloped in its shell, are compelled by the wheel of time to wander within You, like particles of dust blowing about in the sky.'

HEAVENS OF THE EAST

Taoism, or Daoism, is a Chinese philosophical tradition advocating humility and religious piety, and the importance of living in harmony with the *Tao* (the Way). This is the natural order and behaviour of the universe – by learning to integrate oneself with 'the Way' and its seemingly chaotic patterns, one can achieve perfection. In this philosophy, which dates back to at least the fourth century BC, human beings are considered a microcosm of the cyclical universe, and emphasis is placed on the primacy of 'the Way' (rather than on anthropomorphic concepts of God), yet here too there is a concept of paradise, and the approach one must take to find it: the mythical Mount K'unlun.

Two Buddhist cosmological maps of 1830. LEFT: *The stepped map shows a relatively tiny actual world (in green and orange), stuck between seven realms of hell and seven planes of heaven.* RIGHT: *The upper half of this map displays the seven great forests and seven rivers, the Sun God Palace, and the 10,000 mile- (16,100km-) high Great Jambu Tree.*

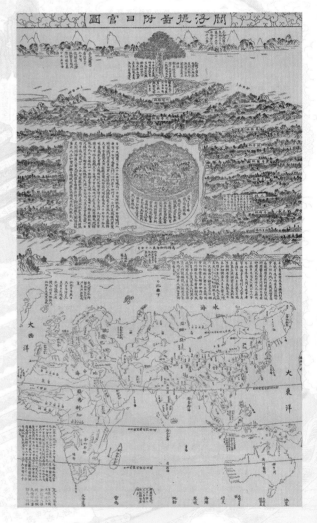

This giant peak is formed of nine levels of different disciplines to master, before one can reach the gateway at its summit that leads to eternal bliss. On entering this paradise, where deathless trees grow and deathless waters flow, you immediately fall under the protection of Xiwangmu, Queen Mother of the West, a goddess with the power to bestow prosperity and longevity on both the living and dead. 'No one knows her beginning; no one knows her end,' writes the Taoist Zhuangzi in the fourth century BC – one of the earliest references to the Queen Mother. According to one Tao legend, she would offer experiences of the joys that await in paradise to members of the living of whom she was most fond, by dispensing a proprietary magic potion.

In contrast, the goal of the Buddhist path is individual liberation from the cycles of rebirth through *nirvana* (extinguishment), reached only when one has managed to put out the 'three fires' or 'three poisons' – *raga* (greed), *dvesha* (aversion) and *moha* (ignorance). Though there have been, and remain, many varying forms of Eastern Buddhism, from those that incorporate spells and sorcery to the rigorous disciplines of Tibetan monastic schools, of particular relevance here is the Ching-tu (Pure Land) school of Buddhism, one of the most widely practised forms in East Asia.

Believers follow the instructions of traditional Buddhism to reach *nirvana*, except for them the goal is a spiritual destination, Sukhavati (the Pure Land) (for there will never be an Earth that is not corrupt), which can be arrived at by also devoting oneself to a later incarnation of the Buddha. This is the Buddha Amitābha (He of Immeasurable Light), who presides over this paradise land that exists somewhere beyond the western sunset. 'If you wish to come and be born in my realm', declares Amitābha in the *Pratyutpanna Samādhi Sūtra*, 'you must always call me to mind again and again, you must always keep this thought in mind without letting up, and thus you will succeed in coming to be born in my realm.' According to another fundamental scripture of the Pure Land faith, the *Sukhāvatīvyūha Sūtra*, it is a fertile place, a wide open plain, mountain-less, crowded with gods and men and filled with flowers, fruits, fragrances and flocks of singing birds: 'When they blow, these breezes scatter flowers all over, filling this buddha-field. These flowers fall into patterns, according to the colours, without ever being mixed up. They have delicate hues

A Tibetan Buddhist mandala of a magical Yantra diagram atop flayed human skin, dated to 1700-1799, used for rituals of magical protection. The image of the skin indicates the spell is to be used with caution.

FOLLOWING PAGE: *An extremely fine embroidered thangka of the Buddhist protective deity Vajrabhairava, made in early fifteenth-century China.*

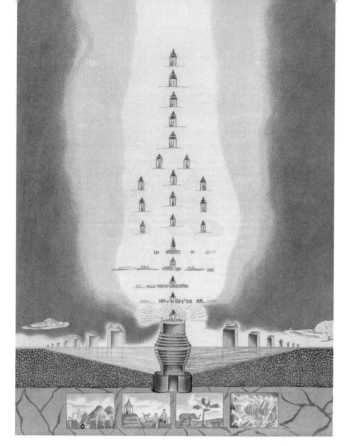

Left: *From* The Thirty-Seven Nats... *by Sir Richard Carnac Temple (1906), the Burmese image of layers of spiritual inhabitations of the earth and heavens. Four infernal regions below the earth; Mount Meru in the centre with its ruby feet; and then the hierarchical layers of the high heavens.*

Below: *A diagram of the Burmese ideas of Sentient Beings, an idea about the evolution of the soul, borrowed from India. It begins in the bottom left with the evil soul in the underworld, until finally in the top-right corner the soul is in the immaterial world, waiting for* nirvana. *From* Thirty-Seven Nats... *(1906).*

A Japanese Taima Mandala of 1750, representing the Pure Land of the Buddha Amitābha, a vast palace on a golden pond.

and strong fragrance. When one steps on these petals, the feet sink 4in [10cm]. When one lifts the foot, the petals return to their original shape and position.'

Streams and rivers, some 50 miles (80km) wide, run through it over golden sands, and as one wades in these waters the temperature of the river adjusts instantly to suit each inhabitant. Sweet-smelling jewel-trees composed of gold, silver, beryl, crystal, coral, red pearls and emeralds line the riverbanks, more precious than any that can be found on Earth, radiating thousands of different colours. Elsewhere grow banana trees, palm trees and fields of lotus flowers also made of precious stones.

Devotees who manage to escape Earth and gain entry to the Pure Lands of Sukhavati, with their confidence in the saving power of Amitābha as their passport, also escape the cycle of rebirth. But this paradise is not necessarily the final destination of these souls – it can be a way station to even higher things, for each soul hears the sounds they wish to hear. These can include lessons in detachment, dispassion, calm and cessation, which can lead one on to the final enlightenment and the ultimate purging of self in *nirvana*.

P'eng-lai was an island believed by the Chinese to exist somewhere in the eastern end of the Bohai Sea, clustered with five others, referred to as the Isles of the Blessed. The legendary paradise was said to hold the elixir of life and inspired search missions ordered by Emperor Ch'in Shih Huang-ti in 219 BC.

GREECE AND ROME: THE GOLDEN AGE, THE ELYSIAN FIELDS AND THE ISLANDS OF THE BLESSED

Far before a yearning for a paradise of the past had European map-makers obsessively charting the Garden of Eden across the seas (see page 15), the ancient Greeks and Romans had their own nostalgic pining for a mythical lost era, a time of immeasurable happiness known as the Golden Age. Writers like Ovid, Hesiod and Plato wax lyrical about this distant time of perfection and divine creation, when the Earth was ruled over by Kronos, father of Zeus, and there was no need for men to work nor women to give birth. Wandering naked, at leisure, enjoying the perfect climate, were humans of such virtue and responsibility that, Plato reports, they were considered by the gods worthy of direct conversation. Nature thrived so ecstatically that bountiful harvests appeared without the need for any cultivation.

There was no need for laws or punishments in the Golden Age, says Ovid in *Metamorphoses*, because people simply did

The Golden Age by Lucas Cranach the Elder. The fortress in the top-left corner could be Hartenfels Castle, residence of the Ernestine dynasty – Cranach's ingratiating way of suggesting their patronage is responsible for a new Golden Age.

SATURNO SUB REGE FUIT GENS AUREA MUNDO,
OMNIA CUI PER SE TERRA INARATA DABAT.
Int vreyeyck had SATURN *sen volck sog rijn als goudt.*
Twelck sonder ploech ghenoot, t'overvuldich gloet der aerden

ÆTAS AUREA

DE GOUDEN EEUW.

ENSIS ERAT NULLUS, NUDOQ SUB ÆTHERE AXE
PACIFICÈ CUIVIS VITA PERACTA FUIT. *R.Iubb.*
Sy wisten van gheen sweert, noch huijs tot hun behoudt,
Maar leefden naackt int velt by leeuwen ende paerden.

the right thing of their own accord. Imagine! The world's
nations existed in perfect harmony, the environment blossomed
in a perpetual spring, and rivers ran with milk and honey.
Death was no more a frightening prospect than falling asleep.
This was during the time of the god Kronos and the Titans,
who would later be overthrown by Zeus and the Olympians.
According to the ancient Greek poet Hesiod this golden race
of men was succeeded by a silver race, then a bronze race, then
a fourth generation who were the magnificent heroes alive in
the time of the Trojan War.

That was *then*, in some long-lost primordial aeon. So,
wondered the Greeks and Romans, was it possible to find that
place and time again? Perhaps a capsule of this golden era
still glimmered somewhere, on some island that time forgot,
virtually unreachable by man. Hesiod explains the land of the
Golden Age could be rediscovered, but one would have to
travel an awful lot farther than to some ocean island, writing
of how Kronos had transferred his kingdom to the underworld
– there, one could find it in the Elysian Fields.

As we have found from exploring the Greco-Roman Hades
earlier in this book, the Greek underworld is a complex
subterranean continent of different zones, or ghost nations.

The Golden Age *by
Antonio Tempesta, 1599.*

Many factors play into the sorting process for new arrivals: one's bravery in life, relation to the gods and a sliding scale of sinfulness. Ultimately, your virtue was your passport. Having been led by Charon the ferryman across the River Styx (with payment provided by the family of the deceased, who placed a coin under the tongue of their loved one), and having successfully passed the hellhound Cerberus, the dead encountered the judges of the underworld. These are usually identified as Aeacus, Rhadamanthus and King Minos, who take the decision as to which region the new applicant should be sent. Tartarus is a boiling hell of punishment; the Mourning Fields, for those who wasted their lives on unrequited love, are comparatively less severe but still not a pleasant place to spend eternity; and the Asphodel Meadows may sound like a relaxing option, but Homer describes them as a dark and mirthless place.

No, it is the rolling hills and lush green valleys of the Elysian Fields, or Elysium (derived from the word meaning 'to be deeply stirred from joy', according to the Byzantine

Charon carries souls across the River Styx *(1861) by Alexander Litovchenko.*

Greek scholar Eustathius of Thessalonica, *c*.1115-1195/6), that is the paradise for which one would hope. There, 'life is easiest for men', writes Homer in the *Odyssey* (4:561 ff.). 'No snow is there, nor heavy storm, nor ever rain, but ever does Ocean send up blasts of the shrill-blowing West Wind that they may give cooling to men.' In the *Aeneid* (6:637), Virgil gives us an idea of how to pass the time in this paradise: 'Here an ampler ether clothes the meads with roseate light, and they know their own sun, and stars of their own. Some disport their limbs on the grassy wrestling-ground, vie in sports, and grapple on the yellow sand; some foot the rhythmic dances and chant poems aloud…' Who could refuse a promise of eternal wrestling, dancing and amateur poetry? 'Each of us suffers his own spirit', writes Virgil in the *Aeneid* (6:742), 'a few of us are later released to wander at will through broad Elysium, the joyous fields; until, in the fullness of time… nothing is left but pure ethereal sentience and the pure flame of the spirit.'

ABOVE: Elysian Fields *by Arthur B. Davies (1862-1928).*

BELOW: *A fresco scene of the god Mercury carrying away dead children in the Elysian Fields, from a* hypogeum *(underground tomb) of the first half of the third century* AD, *discovered in the former Roman township of Ottavia.*

The Greek writer Plutarch (*c.*AD 46–after AD 119) described entry into the fields as a process that followed an initial period of rather apprehensive uncertainty: 'At first one wanders and wearily hurries to and fro, and journeys with suspicion through the dark as one uninitiated: then come all the terrors before the final initiation, shuddering, trembling, sweating, amazement…' Happily, this is eventually followed by one being 'struck with marvellous light, one is received into pure regions and meadows, with voices and dances and the majesty of holy sounds and shapes: among these he who has fulfilled initiation wanders free, and released and bearing his crown joins in the divine communion, and consorts with pure and holy men…'

Depending on the source, the Elysian Fields can be found on an archipelago known as the Islands of the Blessed; or maybe the fields contained the paradise archipelago within the boundary of their netherworld zone. Perhaps, these Isles could even be found on the terrestrial realm; a belief that the Greek historian Plutarch in his *Sertorius* examines and scoffs at: 'A firm belief has made its way, even to the Barbarians, that here is the Elysian Fields and the abode of the blessed which is not true, of which Homer sang.' (Plutarch, *Sertorius*, VIII, 2.)

OPPOSITE: The Embarkation for Cythera *by the French painter Jean-Antoine Watteau, early eighteenth century. Cythera (now Kythira) is an island classically associated with the goddess Venus and a paradise of more erotic nature than Elysium and the Isles of the Blest.*

BELOW: The Waters of Lethe by the Plains of Elysium *(1880) by John Roddam Spencer Stanhope (1829–1908). Lethe (literally 'forgetfulness') is one of the rivers of the ancient underworld, drunk by reincarnated souls to lose the memories of their previous lives. In the background can be seen the happy souls of the Elysian Fields.*

Regardless, over time the number of these islands shrank to just a single Isle of the Blessed, or Fortunate Isle, and while some writers describe the two ideas as separate, others consider the Isles interchangeable with the idea of Elysium itself. 'Those who have persevered three times, on either side, to keep their souls free from all wrongdoing', waxes the poet Pindar, 'follow Zeus's road to the end, to the tower of Kronos, where ocean breezes blow around the island of the blessed, and flowers of gold are blazing.'

BELOW: *The ceiling of the Tomb of the Diver, a fabulously rare survival of ancient Greek painting discovered in 1968 in southern Italy. The diver is considered to be symbolic, representing the moment of death and the plunging of the soul into the sea of eternity.*

MESOAMERICAN HEAVENS

We have seen how widely the vision of a universe structured with thirteen heavens and nine hells is shared between these Classic Mesoamerican civilisations. For the Maya, the thirteen levels of the upper realm and the nine layers of the underworld were all connected by the giant Ceiba tree of the universe, its trunk and branches growing like a spine through all of the spiritual realms with the middle world (Earth) at the centre.

It was an Earth of a tenuous human existence, for the Maya believed in a cosmic cycle of destruction and renewal, and that the gods had previously fashioned mankind in different forms, as explained by the Mayan text *Popol Vuh* (Book of the People). The first men were made from mud, were unable to move and 'spoke but had no mind'. Their dissatisfied creators wiped them out with a flood and returned to the drawing board.

ABOVE: *A Maya burial urn to preserve the bones of one's ancestors. The central scene shows a deceased ruler in a clawed jaguar costume splashed with blood – jaguars were sacred, believed to be mediators between worlds. The lord of the underworld, shown to the right and left, welcomes the figure to his final destination.*

LEFT: *This c.600-900 incense burner depicts the Maya deity Kinich Ahau (Sun Lord), with his trademark nose and shell and fish symbols around his mouth. Smoke and fragrance would have plumed from the face.*

LEFT: *This jaguar-head jar was a luxury item made to be buried with a Maya nobleman or noblewoman in their tomb to provide them with drinking chocolate in the afterlife.* AD *300-600.*

The second race of men were fashioned from trees and the women from reeds. Again, these lacked the intellectual capacity to pay homage to their makers, but were immortal, able to rise from the dead after three days. They too were obliterated, with a flood of boiling water, and the few survivors were believed to be the origins of monkeys. The third were created from yellow and white maize dough and filled with the blood of the gods. Just four dough-men and four dough-women were made, and this time the experiment was *too* successful. The gods found their intelligence to be a threat to their own superiority, and were all set to destroy them as well when Heart of Heaven (the name in the creation story for the god Huracán, whom the *Popol Vuh* implies is a creator god) dulled their minds and dimmed their eyes. Now suitably witless, mankind was born.

It appears that a unified, clearly defined concept of the afterlife probably did not exist among the various groups collectively known as the Maya. The Pokoman Maya of the Verapaz believed their dead king would descend to the previously discussed underworld of Xibalba (page 69). The Yucatec Maya believed in an underworld but also had a system

LEFT: *A* tumi *ceremonial knife used for human sacrifice, from the tenth to twelfth centuries.*

OPPOSITE: *The top of the* Selden Roll, *or* The Roll of the New Fire, *from the first half of the sixteenth century, from Mexico, which shows eight heavens in star-embedded bands (stars are usually represented with eyes). In the ninth heaven, Quetzalcoatl sits between the supreme deity, The Two, who invest him with the power to rule and control the powers of life.*

of judgement – the virtuous were guided to a paradise by the goddess Ixtab. At the Palenque tomb of Pakal the Great, royal Maya ancestors are shown springing up from the soil as fruit trees, together embodying an eternal paradise orchard.

Also within this theme is the common term in Classic Maya iconography that is the Flower Mountain, a living, moving mountain or mountain cave profusely decorated with flower symbols. This icon has been interpreted in several ways: it has been identified with the belief of the present-day Tz'utujil Mayas in a magical mountain that stands at the core of the Earth; as a paradise that is home to the Maya ancestors; as Chicomoztoc, the mythical origin place of all Nahuas (Nahuatl-speaking peoples); and a celestial destination to which ancestors travel to the solar gods. And then there is the suggestion that, far from being a solar paradise, the Flower Mountain could be an aquatic paradise – perhaps an equivalent to Tlālōcān, the Aztec rain god's paradise. This idea was drawn from aquatic imagery and physical remains of marine animals that have been found in numerous Classic Maya tombs.

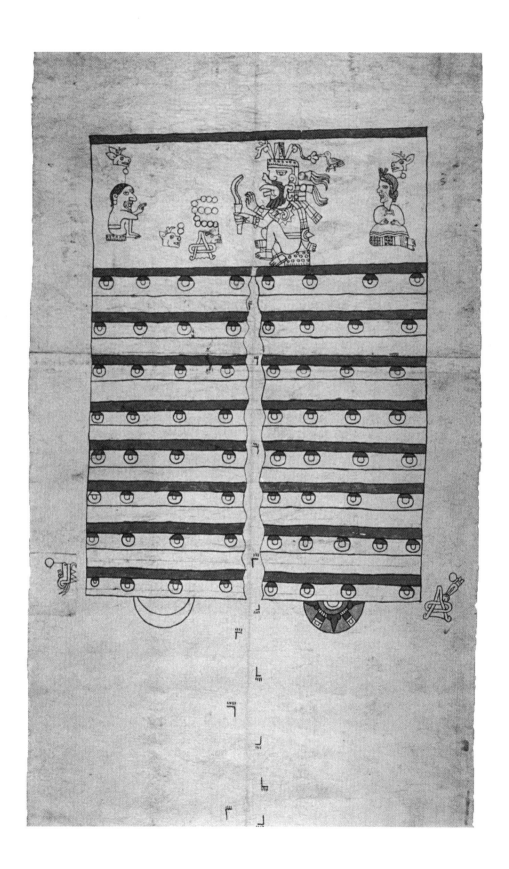

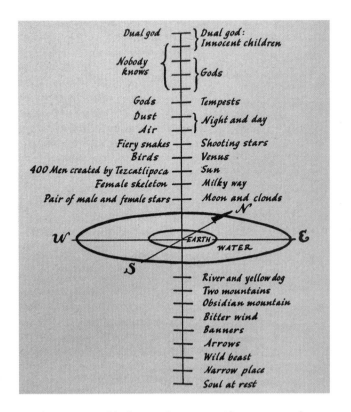

Diagram showing the Nahua cosmology.

The Maya would often use human sacrifice as a way of opening communication with, and paying tribute to, the gods and residents of these colourful heavens. Most frequently, this was done during times of war. The *nacom* (war priest) would hope to elicit divine favour for military victory by sacrificing prisoners of war to satisfy the gods. Prisoners of high rank were reserved as sacrifices to mark prestigious events, such as the coronation of a new king or queen. These killings could be performed in any number of gruesome ways, but the most common were decapitation and heart removal (while the prisoner was alive and conscious), but more popular was to throw the prisoner into a cenote (deep natural well) to die a slow death. In fact, this last method was also used to open up a line of communication with heaven: Maya children were sometimes gently lowered down into these wells and left alone for long periods of time so that they would converse with the gods. Hours later, the children were pulled back up so that the divine messages they were expected to have received could be delivered.

For the Inca, the antipode to the murky *ukhu pacha* (world below) was the high realm of *hana pacha* (world above), Land

of the Sun, home to the stars, planets and the gods, where virtuous Inca could spend their days enveloped in divine solar warmth. The most important of the resident deities are: Inti the sun god (from whom the Inca believed their king, the Sapa Inca, was descended); Mama Killa, the moon goddess; and Illapa, the god of thunder and lightning, who was said to be a man in shining clothes who carried a club and stored the Milky Way in a jug to make rain.

Rainbows and lighting bolts served as magical routes from the terrestrial to the celestial realm, while mountain peaks were considered sacred heavenly doorways and were the locations for ritual sacrifices (including human sacrifice) to the gods. The virtuous deceased were able to make use of these divine highways at their leisure, once they considered their business on Earth concluded. It was important, though, to protect the departed's body – death forced the soul from the body, but both continued to live on, with the same needs as before. It was thought that if the body was destroyed then the soul would be doomed to wander

A mural unearthed in the 1940s at Teotihuacan, interpreted by the archaeologist Alfonso Caso as showing a Teotihuacan equivalent of the paradise of Tlālōcān, with the central figures identified as an equivalent of Tlaloc, the Mesoamerican god of rain and warfare. It's now thought that this is a female deity of the afterlife, labelled the Teotihuacan Spider Woman by the Mesoamericanist Karl Taube.

aimlessly on Earth, and so great care was put into preparing the corpse in its tomb, so that the soul would reach its heavenly destination and in turn assist those who had cared for it.

In the Aztec belief system (or more specifically, the Nahua people, which includes the Aztecs, Chichimecas and the Toltecs), the thirteen-layer heavenly structure is articulated with particular detail. Each level was ruled over by different 'Lords' (gods), with the structure of the Thirteen Heavens as a whole formed out of the head of Cipactli, the primordial cosmic crocodile whose body the gods used as the basis of creation. (Tlaltícpac, the Earth, was carved from Cipactli's core, while the nine layers of the underworld Mictlān were made from its tail.)

In terms of paradise destinations for the soul, only a few are of relevance here. The lowest heaven is Ilhuicatl-Meztli (sky where the moon moves). Here live the gods Meztli, the moon goddess; Tlazolteotl, goddess of lust and adultery; Tlaloc, god of thunder, who stabs the bellies of clouds to produce rain; and Ehecatl, Lord of the Wind, who drives clouds with his breath. Though a place of low order, this level of heaven is a realm of

Figures swim in criss-crossed rivers flowing from a mountain, a scene interpreted by the archaeologist Alfonso Caso as being of the afterlife realm of Tlaloc.

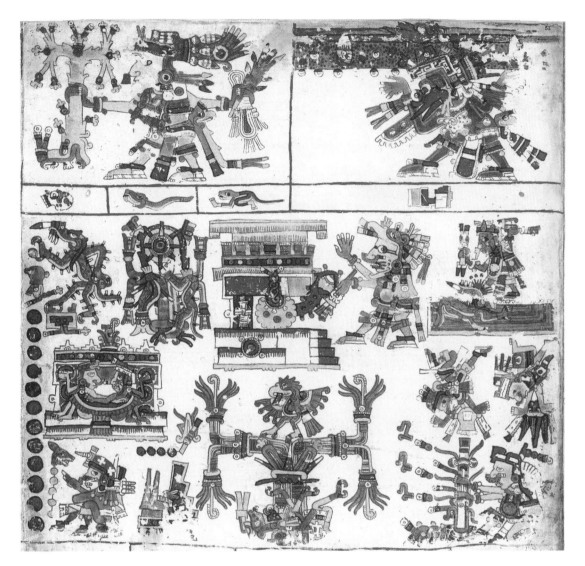

happiness. As the missionary priest Bernardino de Sahagún (1499-1590) mentions in *Historia de las Cosas de Nueva España*: 'There the ears of green corn are never lacking, nor calabashes, sprays of grass, green pepper, tomatoes, beans green in the husk, and flowers, and there live gods called Thaloques, who appear to minister to the idols, who wear their hair long...'

With Tlaloc in residence, this lowest land of plenty is also known as Tlālōcān (Land of Water and Mist). To Tlālōcān travel the souls of those who have drowned, or been struck by lightning, the physically deformed or those who died of illnesses related to the rain deity and whose miserable death ensures they are now under the special care of the god of water.

Tlahuiztlampa (direction of the place of dawn), the eastern region of the afterlife where one can receive the advice of ancestors and connect with the Eastern guardian Quetzalcoatl, the flying plumed snake deity.

Flowers adorn this heaven as profusely as in the afterworlds of the Maya – when a new soul arrives in this land of mist, dry branches immediately burst into bloom, ushering the visitor into a land of perpetual spring. The newcomer breaks into a song of gratitude to Tlālōcān, before joining in with football games, leapfrogging or lazing in the shade on a bed of flowers besides streams. After four years of this constant joy, the soul returns to the land of the living. Meanwhile, all other mortals have to go to the Mictlān underworld.

Also of interest is the third heaven, Ilhuicatl-Tonatiuh (where the sun moves), which is home to Tonatiuh, god of the Fifth Sun. It is a realm profuse with flowers, birds and butterflies, the destination for the spirits of men killed in battle and of women who die in childbirth. The former escort the Sun along its flower road to its zenith, before handing over to the women, who accompany it to its setting point. Both perform this guardian duty in the form of flowers, bright-feathered birds and butterflies.

The highest heaven is Ilhuicatl-Omeyocan (Place of Two or Place of Duality), home to the creator couple, the deities Ometecuhtli, god of sustenance and the cycle of life, and his female counterpart Omecihuatl. In this golden realm, the dual god-goddess is / are joined by the souls of children who have died before they developed faculties of reason, nourished by the milk that drips from the branches of an ever-blossoming tree. The children have the striking chromatic appearance of jade, turquoise and glittering jewels and, in their communion with the great creators in a land of beauty and innocence, are safe from ever having to travel to the cold land of the dead.

Following the Spanish conquest such beliefs were not extinguished but rather incorporated into the Christian story, the paradise worlds associated with Catholic heaven. This we can see from the following fragment of a post-conquest poem recited by young Nahua children to the Virgin Mary:

Like a quetzal feather we return to earth,
we, the little children, and we humble ourselves,
praying to Saint Mary, always a Virgin.
Like many-coloured feathers we are tinted;
Like a necklace of pearls we are strung:
we, the little children,
praying to Saint Mary, always a Virgin.

OPPOSITE: *An ángel arcabucero (arquebusier angel) of the Cusco School, a tradition of magnificent artworks that depict Catholic angels dressed in the style of Andean nobles and armed with arquebuses (an early muzzle-loaded, long gun). This helped integrate Catholic religion with the indigenous belief systems.*

JANNAH: THE ISLAMIC GARDEN PARADISE

Two illustrations from a Uyghur manuscript of the Nahj al-Faradis*, commissioned by Sultan Abu Sa'id Gurkan c.1465, depicting the heavens shown to the Prophet Muhammad (not pictured) on his night journey.*

The key to understanding the original power of the Islamic image of paradise is to consider the fact that the Arabian Peninsula, at some 1,250,000 sq. miles (2,600,000 sq. km), is the largest region in the world to not have a single river. How wondrous, then, the lush aquatic delights of Jannah, the Islamic paradise. Should you possess sufficient righteousness to traverse successfully from the limbo state of Barzakh across the As-Sirāt bridge (which, for sinners, narrows to the uncrossable width of a human hair), you find yourself welcomed at the gates of Jannah by a whooping chorus of angels crying 'Peace be with you, that you persevered in patience! Now how excellent is the final home!' (Qur'an 13:24.) It's a buzzing, multilayered afterworld crammed with tents, pavilions and marketplaces. There you find what is simply known as the Garden, one of a number of verdant areas of perpetual bliss, full of flowing rivers, with subdivision gardens described as being as wide as the heavens and Earth (Qur'an 3.133). Each landscape accords a blessed resident with a mansion, decorated with sofas, carpets, goblets of wine and spreads of meat and fruit for indulgent relaxation. There is no text that provides an explicit tour of the Islamic paradise; but, as with Jahannam (the fire), the Qur'an

mentions numerous details that are built on in the Hadiths
to paint a detailed picture. In fact, the paradise of Jannah is
covered in even greater detail in texts than its counterpart
hell, which is quite unusual. At the same time, Muhammad
tells us that the wonders of the Garden are ultimately beyond
description: 'Allah has said: "I have prepared for My righteous
servants what no eye has seen, what no ear has heard, and what
no heart has conceived" '. The Qur'an also states: 'No person
knows what is kept hidden for them of delights of the eye as a
reward for what they used to do' (Qur'an 32:17.) The pleasures
of paradise are inconceivable to the human mind.

So what clues do we have as to the architecture and geography
of the realm? According to the Islamic scholar al-Tirmidhi
(824-892), when the prophet was asked about the buildings that

*The magnificent paradise
garden of Shah 'Abbas I
(r. 1588-1629), one of the
great kings of the Persian
Safavid dynasty (1501-1736).*

The Prophet Muhammad (not pictured) encounters the Angel of Half Fire Half Snow. From an Iranian manuscript of c.1465.

stood in paradise, he replied: 'Bricks of gold and silver, and mortar of fragrant musk, pebbles of pearl and sapphire, and soil of saffron. Whoever enters it is filled with joy and will never feel miserable; he will live there forever and never die; their clothes will never wear out and their youth will never fade.'

According to the Islamic text *The Book Pertaining to Paradise, Its Description, Its Bounties, and Its Intimates*, for each of the faithful there is a giant tent formed of a single, giant, hollowed-out pearl 60 miles (100km) wide: 'In paradise there is a street to which [the blessed] will come every Friday. The north wind will blow and will scatter fragrance on their faces and on their clothes and will add to their beauty and loveliness, and they will go back to their families after having an added lustre to their beauty and loveliness.'

Rivers flow through, and under, the Garden – in fact in the Qur'an Jannah is frequently referred to as the 'gardens beneath which rivers flow' (Qur'an 47:12), for nothing could be a more pleasant contrast to the reality of those living on the arid Arabian Peninsula. But there weren't just rivers of water – the Qur'an mentions rivers of fresh milk, wine and honey: 'Here is a parable of the Garden, which the righteous are promised: in it are rivers of water; incorruptible rivers of milk of which the taste never changes; rivers of wine, a joy to those who drink; and rivers of honey pure and clear.' (Qur'an 47:15.) (The notion of four rivers corresponds with the four rivers associated with the Garden of Eden in Genesis, named Pishon, Gihon,

The gigantic Rooster Angel of Prayer, so large that its head reaches God's throne while its feet rest on the earth. The angel Jibril explains that the mega-fowl is the angel that keeps track of time and calls the faithful to prayer.

Hiddekel and Phirat.) In Hadiths, these rivers grow to enormous size, and al-Firdaws (the highest level of heaven) is described as having one hundred levels of roaring torrents.

In the *Islamic Book of the Dead*, we are informed of the weekly routine of the blissful dead who drink from these rivers: on Saturday they drink water, on Sunday liquid honey. Monday is milk. Wine is drunk on Tuesday, and after becoming intoxicated the dead take flight for one thousand years, until they reach an enormous mountain of pure, aromatic musk, where they drink the sweet water *salsabil* on Wednesday. They then reach a high castle and recline on couches to drink ginger on Thursday, and eventually end up at the Table of Immortality to drink nectar.

Drunkenness, though, isn't so much of a problem with the wine of paradise, which will never sour and leads only to pleasure and no hangover: 'There will be circulated among them a cup [of wine] from a flowing spring. White and delicious to the drinkers. No bad effect is there in it…' (Qur'an 37:45-47).

When the prophet was asked how people relieve themselves in heaven, he answered: 'They relieve themselves by perspiring through their skins, and its fragrance will be that of musk, and all stomachs will have become lean' (Ibn Hibban).

Jannah is also a landscape of titanic, magical flora that offer cool shade and endless fruit. (One tradition reports that when the trees knock against each other they strike a beautiful note.) While exploring Jahannam earlier in this book we came across the hell-tree Zaqqum – in Jannah it has a few counterparts. The giant and mysterious Sidraï al-Muntahā (Lote-Tree of the Utmost Farthest Boundary), for one, looms at the far end of the Garden, near the abode of Allah himself (Qur'an 53:20), marking the boundary of heaven, a border that no creation can cross.

There is also the enormous tree known as Tūbā (Blessedness), a term mentioned only once in the Qur'an but again in the Hadiths, that over the years inspired writers like Sohrevardi to suggest it to be a tree in heaven where the mythical bird Simurgh (equivalent to a griffin) lay its eggs. Abu Hurairah reports Muhammad as saying: 'In paradise, there is a tree under the shadow of which a rider can travel for a hundred years.'

Islamic Jannah was portrayed as a markedly more sensual and erotic realm in comparison with the contemporary descriptions of the Christian paradise, where the severity of asceticism had taken hold. The best-known feature of paradise in this vein are the houris, which in Islamic tradition are the virginal maidens awaiting the virtuous in paradise. 'Surely for the god-fearing awaits a place of security, gardens and vineyards, and maidens with swelling breasts, like of age' (Sura 78:33 of the Qur'an). The beautiful houris are magnificent as rubies, beautiful as coral, chaste as hidden pearls, and are mentioned in several passages of the Qur'an, always in plural form. (No specific number is ever given in the Qur'an for the number of houris accompanying each believer.) They are 'companions' (Qur'an 36:55), 'with large and beautiful eyes' (Qur'an 37:48), described in Hadiths as 'transparent to the marrow of their bones', 'eternally young', 'hairless except the eyebrows and the head', 'pure' and 'beautiful'.

According to the *Islamic Book of the Dead* they were quite colourful in appearance: 'The Prophet said: "Allah-ta-'ala created the faces of houris of four colours: white, green, yellow and red. He created their bodies of saffron, musk, amber and camphor." ' It certainly is a realm of enjoyment, as the same

source continues: 'The people of the Garden increase in beauty and handsomeness every day… One man is given the power of one hundred in eating, drinking and sexual enjoyment.'

Western visitors to Islamic lands were so taken by the sensual elements of Jannah that exaggerated versions circulated throughout thirteenth-century Europe, most significantly in the *Liber Scalae Machometi* (Book of Muhammad's Ladder), in 1264. This caused a sensation with its intoxicating visions of overflowing feasting tables, emerald- and pearl-covered pavilions and ruby-encrusted palaces full of willing virgins. So flushed were the popular fantasies of Western Christendom by this colour-boosted idea of paradise that we can see its influence on separate medieval European fantasylands, such as the dreamland of Cockaigne, explored later (see page 230), an imaginary paradise of plenty that lived as shared dream for centuries.

'A simurgh and an army of birds attack the spirit of the ocean.' From a nineteenth-century illuminated copy of the Persian mythical work Anvār-i Suhaylī *(The Lights of Canopus).*

VALHALLA

Spending eternity joyfully hacking at one's friends with a longsword might not, I would venture, be the average person's idea of paradise; but then the Viking warrior could hardly be described as the average person. For the Norsemen, the magnificent paradise of Valhalla (from the Old Norse *Valhöll*, the hall of the slain), Odin's house of heroes, was all about indulgence.[1] It is a hard-earned reward, though – Odin and his Valkyries only grant entrance to those who have fought courageously and died in battle. (There are other references that show dead warriors can also occasionally be sent to Hel, too. The chronicler Snorri Sturluson claims that only those who die of illness or old age go to Hel, but he then contradicts himself when telling the story of Baldr, son of Odin, who dies a warrior's death yet is sent to Hel regardless.)

An enormous, ornate banquet hall guarded by wolves and encircled by eagles, the 'gold-bright' Valhalla features a roof made from battle shields, with rafters formed of spears, and the seating around the many long dining tables fashioned from breastplates. The dead guests of Valhalla are known as the *einherjar*, and spend their time doing all of the things

OPPOSITE: *Valhalla (left) and Jörmungandr (right), the gigantic Midgard Serpent, fished from the oceans using an ox head. From a seventeenth-century Icelandic manuscript.*

---

1 There's also the theory that Valhalla being a hall might be mistranslation. In Swedish folklore, there are mentions of mountains believed to house the dead that were also called *Valhall* – perhaps therefore the noun *höll* derives from *hallr* (rock), and Valhalla was originally an entire underworld, not a hall.

BELOW: Valhalla *(1896) by Max Brückner.*

they enjoyed doing in their terrestrial time – namely fighting, feasting, drinking and more fighting, with the occasional act of valour before another brawl.[2] This can be enjoyed to an endless degree, because each evening their wounds are magically healed and they are returned to full health ready for the next bout.

This regenerative magic is also utilised in the kitchens: the dinner meat is stripped from the great boar Sæhrímnir, who returns to life every time he is slaughtered and butchered. For something to wash it down, one can wander over to the goat Heiðrún and its tireless udders, from which can be squeezed a delicious mead that fills a vat large enough to satiate every warrior in the place. There is also the deer Eikþyrnir, whose antlers feed liquid into the spring Hvergelmir, from which burst forth numerous rivers. ('The young stag, drenched in dew, who surpasses all other animals, and whose horns glow against the sky itself,' goes stanza 38 of the poem *Helgakviða Hundingsbana II*, found in the Old Norse collection the *Poetic Edda*.) Table service in Valhalla is provided by a bevy of beautiful Valkyries.

For further descriptions we can also turn to the poem 'Grímnismál' in the *Poetic Edda*. In stanzas 8-10, Odin reports that Valhalla is located in the realm of Glaðsheimr ('bright home' in Old Norse), describing how the hall is shining and golden and 'rises peacefully' when seen from a distance. Later in the poem we learn of the colossal outer gate of Valhalla, Valgrind (Death-gate), which 'is the lattice called, in the plain that stands, holy before the holy gates: ancient is that lattice, but few only know how it is closed with lock'. Within the security of Valgrind, Valhalla itself has 540 gates, each large

ABOVE: *The Tjängvide image stone, a Viking Age image stone from c.1000 at Tjängvide, Sweden. It is believed to depict Odin astride his eight-legged horse Sleipnir (or possibly a dead warrior riding his horse), as he welcomes brave warriors to Valhalla.*

LEFT: *A coloured version of Denmark's tenth-century Jelling Runestone depicting the Crucifixion. This image of Christ is thought to indicate the parallels with the 'hanging' of the Norse god Odin from a tree, and being pierced by a spear.*

---

2 For more information on the brutal activities that the Vikings considered leisure activities, such as 'skin-pulling' and 'recreational drowning', see Brooke-Hitching, E. (2015) *Fox Tossing, Octopus Wrestling and Other Forgotten Sports*, London: Simon & Schuster.

enough for 800 men to rush from at once. Valhalla is so massive as to contain many giant subdivision halls, like Bilskirnir, Thor's hall, which has 540 rooms and is considered by Odin grandest of all. We also learn from Odin that the grazing ground of the goat Heiðrún and the hart Eikþyrnir is on top of Valhalla as they chew on the branches of the tree Læraðr.

A curious feature discovered in recent archaeological unearthing of Viking warrior graves has led to the development of a theory that our image of how the Vikings perceived the afterlife should be, literally, reversed. In 2020, archaeologists in Norway, headed by Raymond Sauvage at the Norwegian University of Science and Technology, uncovered the 1100-year-old grave of a Viking warrior and found that he had been laid with his sword carefully placed on his left side, not the usual right. 'The idea is that this placement must reflect some beliefs that were important in the mortuary rites,' Sauvage told journalists, adding that 'other [Viking] items are often found to be placed mirrored of what is normal. Several archaeologists therefore believe that this may reflect a belief that they understood the afterlife to be mirrored of the normal world.'

We also glean another curious sword detail from the beginning of 'Skáldskaparmál', the second part of Snorri Sturluson's *Prose Edda*. Here the author beats George Lucas to the idea of a 'light-sabre' by at least 800 years, with an account of the revellers using glowing swords as their sole source of light while they drink, in a hall – later confirmed as Valhalla in Chapter 22 – with walls covered with beautiful shields. The heroes of Valhalla rejoice and feast until the inevitable Doomsday of Ragnarök approaches, at which point the warriors will charge from the 540 doors and take their place in Odin's forces, to fight the giants and the wolf Fenrir, a battle that they are expected to lose. This is their last act of valour, and the ultimate point of Valhalla – for Odin to collect the best fighters for his last great battle.

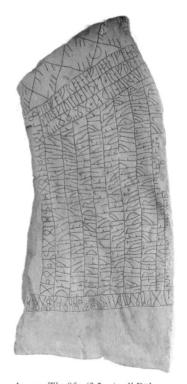

Above: *The 8ft- (2.5m-) tall Rök runestone. A recent Swedish study suggested it to be a memorial to a 'death-doomed' man named Vamoth, who perished and joined Odin's army to fight against the giants and the wolf Fenrir, swallower of the Sun.*

BIBLICAL HEAVEN

Across the millennia, there have been Jewish groups who have believed in a variety of forms of afterlife. The early rabbis taught that those who diligently followed the Halakhah (the name for rabbinic law) would receive rewards in a world yet to come, called Olam Ha-Ba, though this is not mentioned in the Hebrew Bible. Some believed that, following the coming of the Messiah, there would be a resurrection of the dead who would face judgement, receiving punishment or reward for their behaviour in life – but there was no explicit teaching on the precise nature of a heaven or a hell. If one was to summarise these centuries of discussion and the principal lessons of Judaism, it could be to say that ultimately the importance is placed on how we live our earthly lives, rather than on the destination following death. The latter is in God's hands – it is impossible for mortals to know what the next world is like. To quote the Mishnah, the first major collection of Jewish oral traditions: 'Be not like servants who serve their master for the sake of receiving a reward' (*Ethics of the Fathers* 1:3). Do good for the sake of doing good.

So, what references are there in the Bible that contribute to the image of heaven in the minds of Christians? On reflection, it might be agreed that as bright as that image is in the modern mind, it is ultimately harder to imagine specific details, other than pearly gates and streets of gold, than say the fiery wastelands of hell. This is partly because, according to Christian theology, the mortal mind is simply incapable of conceiving its true grandeur.

St Augustine of the fifth century described heaven as 'ineffable' – beyond words. See 1 Corinthians 2:9: 'What no eye has seen, nor ear heard, nor the heart of man conceived, what God has prepared for those who love him.' This is the medieval Catholic concept of heaven, the *visio beatifica* (beatific vision), or the sight of God, a full knowledge of God that one will only obtain in heaven. As Paul states about the concept that would later be developed into that of the *visio beatifica*, on Earth 'now we see through a glass, darkly', but in the hereafter 'face to face. Now I know in part; then I shall understand fully, even as I have been fully understood' (1 Corinthians 13:12).

Above: *The Creator, with the angels of heaven above and the gaping jaw of hell below. From the* Holkham Bible Picture Book, *an English manuscript of c.1327-1335.*

Opposite: Map of the Kingdom of Heaven *(1650) by Nicolas Cochin. A religious broadside showing the division between heaven, purgatory and hell. The walled celestial city of Jerusalem is at the top; the souls of purgatory are shown below, beyond the gates of heaven; and then the flaming rivers of hell ruled by Lucifer are at the bottom.*

Trinité

le Royeaume des Cieux.

Cherubins

Vertus

les *Saincts*

le

Puissances

Principautes

Dominations

Throsnes

Archanges

la S.te Cité de

Anges

Ierusalem Celeste

le Purgatoire

le Purgatoire

le Monde

le Royaume d'Enfer

Par Permission
& Priuilege du Roy,
Octroié a lauteur, lequel la cedé à
Pierre Mariette demeurant ruë sainct
Iacques a l'Esperance.
Auec approbation de M.rs les Docteurs de Sorbonne.

Cette Carte du
Royaume des Cieux a esté
composée par le S. Hierosme Chastelain

A la gloire de Dieu Roy des Roys.

A PARIS

Deprivation of this vision was the worst torture imaginable, labelled by the learned of the Middle Ages as *poena damni* (punishment of the damned), a key component of hell.

St Paul clarifies that 'the kingdom of God does not mean food and drink but righteousness and peace and the Holy Spirit' (Romans 14:17). Early theologians and preachers had to fight constantly to reinforce the idea that this paradise on Earth established by God (for only later would the idea of a celestial heaven as destination for the virtuous to join God be developed) was essentially an improved version of life on Earth.

In Judaism, Abba Arikha (AD 175-247) said of the world to come: 'There is there neither eating, nor drinking, nor any begetting of children, no bargaining or jealousy or hatred or strife. All that the righteous do is to sit with their crowns on their heads and enjoy the effulgence of the Presence' (*Encyclopaedia Judaica* xii, 1357). Heaven, for Jesus, was ultimately oneness with God, and he provides few specific details, though according to John's Gospel at the Last Supper he promised his apostles everlasting life with the words: 'In my Father's house are many mansions: if it were not so, I would have told you. I go to prepare a place for you' (John 14:2).

As with hell, we find the most vivid, definitive and enduring imagery of heaven disclosed to St John as reported in Revelation. A door is opened in heaven, and through it John is brought. He finds a place reminiscent of a grand imperial court, in the process of a liturgical ceremony. A figure with the appearance of jasper and carnelian sits on a throne that emits lightning and thunder, encircled by a rainbow, and surrounded by four living beasts in the forms of a lion, an ox, a man and an eagle. Each have six wings and are covered with eyes all over their body. These are the Cherubim, who chant endlessly 'Holy,

The archangel Michael, symbol of the triumph over evil. The Antichrist lies at his feet, cast out of heaven.

IN PARALIPMENON LIBRO SCDO

The heavenly Jerusalem as a city, from the Liber Floridus *(Book of Flowers), c.1200.*

holy, holy, Lord God Almighty, which was, and is, and is to come.' (Early on in Christian thought, these four beings were interpreted as representing the four evangelists Matthew, Mark, Luke and John.)

Later, in Revelation 21, the New Jerusalem is seen descending to Earth 'prepared as a bride adorned for her husband' from God – a magnificent, celestial city that will be the terrestrial residence of, and temple to, God. So bright will His light be as it streams through the golden streets that no light from the sun nor moon is needed. It is a dazzling city made of precious stones:

And the building of the wall of it was of jasper: and the city was pure gold, like unto clear glass. And the foundations of the wall of the city were garnished with all manner of precious stones. The first foundation was jasper; the second, sapphire; the third, a chalcedony; the fourth, an emerald; the fifth, sardonyx; the sixth, sardius; the seventh, chrysolyte; the eighth, beryl; the ninth, a topaz; the tenth, a chrysoprasus; the eleventh, a jacinth; the twelfth, an amethyst

Revelation 21:18-20

John is carried to a high mountain and shown a view overlooking the heavenly city. From this vantage point, John goes into detail about the actual measurements of the city: 'And the city lieth foursquare, and the length is as large as the breadth: and he measured the city with the reed, twelve thousand furlongs. The length and the breadth and the height of it are equal' (Revelation 21:15-16). Its great high walls are encrusted with jewels, and its twelve gates are each made from a single giant pearl. Its saved inhabitants need never fear anything again: 'And God shall wipe away all tears from their eyes; and there shall be no more death, neither sorrow, nor crying, neither shall there be any more pain: for the former things are passed away' (Revelation 21:4). And in the centre: 'In the midst of the street of it, and on either side of the river, was there the tree of life, which bare twelve manner of fruits, and yielded her fruit every month: and the leaves of the tree were for the healing of the nations' (Revelation 22:2).

A twelfth-century icon depicting the thirty-step ladder to heaven described in the seventh-century work The Ladder of Divine Ascent *or* The Ladder of Paradise *by St John Climacus, a monk of Mount Sinai. Each rung represents a Christian virtue, as devils drag followers down to hell.*

These scriptural references to a heavenly Kingdom of
God on Earth were to be taken absolutely literally, according
to one distinguished early Christian thinker, St Irenaeus
(c. AD 130-c.202), bishop of the Roman city of Lugdunum
(modern Lyon) in Gaul. Irenaeus – polemically – insisted
on literal interpretation over allegorical reading, and believed
in a relatively sensual and almost karmic-like compensatory
nature of the heaven on Earth that will come with the return
of Christ to 'destroy temporal kingdoms and bring in the
eternal one' – the kingdom of the Messiah.

Angel of the Revelation *by
William Blake, c.1803-1805.
Inspired by Revelation, Chapter
10. St John gazes at a 'mighty
angel... clothed with a cloud...
a rainbow was upon his head,
and his face was as it were the
sun, and his feet as pillars of fire.'*

Give a poor man a meal, for example, and you will be rewarded with one hundred meals of your own, each one hundred times more delicious than you have tasted, in this eventual kingdom of the Messiah. The meek shall not only inherit the earth but shall live blissfully off it, in the kind of paradise of material and sensual delights that Christians would come to condemn Muslims for their belief in. There one can drink the fruit of the vine, for 'the resurrection shall be flesh', in a terrestrial heaven where: 'Vineyards shall grow, having each 10,000 main shoots: and in one main shoot 10,000 branches, and in one branch again 10,000 sprigs, and upon every sprig 10,000 clusters, and every grape when pressed shall yield twenty-five measures of wine. And when any of those saints shall lay hold of a cluster, another cluster shall exclaim, I am a better cluster, take me' (Irenaeus, *Against Heresies c.*180).

While details of heaven are occasionally provided in the Old and New Testaments, it is with relative vagueness as to exactly where it is and what one would find there. Revelation, in contrast, provides an almost diagrammatic street plan complete with measurement – but what of daily life there? For centuries, writers scoured texts and extrapolated with their own logic to attempt to provide answers. What colours, sounds, tastes and other terrestrial features should one expect to find? Well, palm trees, for one, writes Lactantius (260-325), adviser to the first Christian Roman emperor, Constantine I. Lactantius introduced the palm tree to heaven, through the association of the Roman palm of victory and the palm branches laid on the ground for Jesus's triumphal entry into Jerusalem on the back of a donkey.

It was also known that God and heaven were beyond time, for in the Second Epistle of Peter it's mentioned that 'with the Lord one day is as a thousand years, and a thousand years as one day' (2 Peter 3:8). Therefore, in heaven there is no day or night, no seasons, no years or centuries. Everything happens and is experienced at once. 'Now, nothing *fades*', confirms the seventeenth-century Anglican preacher Lancelot Andrewes, 'but all springs fresh and green. At this time, here; but at all times there: a perpetual spring; no other season there, but that' (J. W. Blench, *Preaching in England*, 1965). (Timelessness is not unique to Christianity – in the Egyptian *Book of the Dead*, for example, the dead man traditionally identifies with Osiris, declares himself to be yesterday, today and tomorrow.)

And unlike the more sensual promises of other paradises, there is no sex in heaven (and therefore nor should there be on Earth), reported Cyprian, the first African bishop, martyred in 258. The good Christian should live a chaste life to achieve the entrance requirement of angelic purity: 'While you remain chaste and virginal, you are equal to the angels of God', he writes. In his treatise *De Paradiso* (On Paradise), St Ambrose, fourth-century Bishop of Milan, agreed with this: 'For chastity', he writes, 'has made even angels. He who has preserved it is an angel; he who has lost it is a devil.'

Almost thirteen hundred years later, in 1698, the Puritan John Dunton wrote *An Essay Proving We Shall Know Our Friends in Heaven*, stating that he would be reunited with his recently deceased wife by God in heaven, but there would be no sexual bond between them. Should anything unchaste take place: 'the angels couldn't stand long but would certainly be seduced from their innocence and fall as Adam did'.

Perhaps there is also no laughter to be found there, either. One striking part of the *Regula Sancti Benedicti* (Rule of Saint Benedict) of the Italian Benedict of Nursia (480-547) is when he, like Perpetua, draws on the image of the ladder to heaven from the dream of Jacob in Genesis 28:12: 'And he dreamed, and behold a ladder set up on the earth, and the top of it

ABOVE: *A map of salvation with elements of paradise, redemption, sacraments, heaven and hell. From a Carthusian miscellany of poems, chronicles and treatises in northern English, created sometime between 1460 and 1500.*

OPPOSITE TOP: The Neville of Hornby Hours *manuscript created c.1325-1375, integrating the ancient Greek idea of the celestial spheres with Christian notions. Angels falling from grace turn into the devils of hell.*

OPPOSITE BOTTOM: *In her* Sci Vias Domini *(Know the Ways of the Lord), Hildegard of Bingen describes twenty-six of her visions, including the one shown here, in which God showed her the universe as taking the shape of a 'cosmic egg'.*

reached to heaven; and behold the angels of God ascending and descending on it.' Benedict attributes qualities to each rung that one must achieve to join the angels on the ascent to heaven. Selflessness and patience, to be sure, but the tenth rung, he writes, represents the absence of laughter. 'The fool raises his voice in laughter', Benedict cautions, rendering his particular heaven rather a dour place.

St Augustine, Bishop of Hippo Regius in Numidia, Roman North Africa, was one of the most important Church Fathers of the Latin Church. His *City of God* is a cornerstone of Western thought, a riposte to the allegation that it was Christianity that brought about the decline of Rome. In it, he examines many profound questions of theology, like the suffering of the virtuous and the existence of evil, but also the practicalities of heaven. Augustine believed in the Resurrection of the physical body that would ascend to heaven once the Devil had been defeated (against the Platonists, who claimed that being earthly the body could not be lifted to the lighter heavens).

Augustine covers the questions of what this would mean for people whose bodies had rotted to dust, whose bodies were consumed by sea, fire or wild animals with one idea: every resurrected person shall take the physical form at the same age, 'the same prime of life', as Christ. Even those who died as children will find miraculous maturity.

The Renaissance artist Fra Angelico's Last Judgement, *painted sometime between 1425 and 1431, now in the museum of San Marco, Florence. One of the first depictions of heaven as a beautiful garden.*

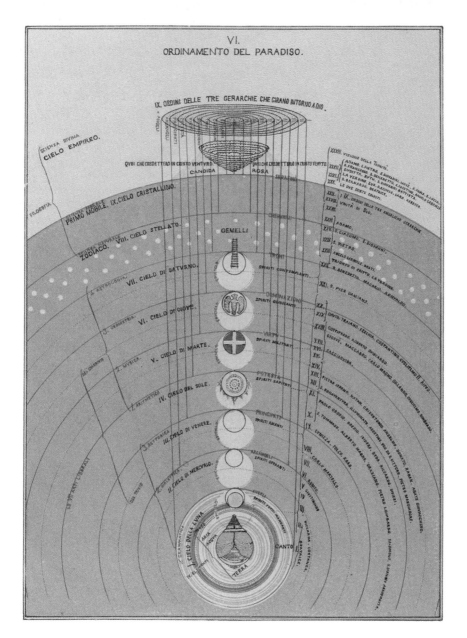

Augustine also addresses a question of his contemporaries – will women also be found in resurrected form in God's Kingdom? This query originated in woman being made out of man, for therefore, in perfection, would not women become men? No, argues Augustine, 'a woman's sex is not a defect; it is natural', and in the afterlife they 'will be free of the necessity of intercourse and childbirth'. Elsewhere, Augustine discusses how in paradise our liver and other organs will become transparent (as we completely reveal ourselves to God), which, he adds, makes not having to eat there all the more fortunate. There is no flatulence in heaven either, he explains, because under the gaze of God even bowels are rendered perfect.

Michelangelo Caetani's 1855 map of the universe of Dante's Divine Comedy, *with the inverse cone of the layers of heaven capped by the Empyrean realm of God at the top.*

A number of the medieval mystics who reported divine
visions and spiritual tours of heaven and hell were women
religious. Some were anchorites, living and working within
sealed walled-in cells, within churches or monasteries.
Distractions and comforts were reduced to a minimum with
little food and exercise. Prayer was the sustenance, as they
attempted to be as close to heaven as humanly possible. Pope
Urban II issued a charter in 1095 encouraging respect for these
women who were 'dead to the world' in order to find their
'eternal spouse'.

The most famous of these visionaries is Hildegard of Bingen
(1098-1179), a German Benedictine abbess, writer and mystic,
whose ecstatic visions came to her when she was awake. She
describes one glimpse of heaven's inhabitants in *Liber vitae
meritorum* (The Book of the Rewards of Life): 'I saw certain
ones, as if through a mirror, who were clothed with the whitest
garment interwoven with gold and embellished with the most
precious stones from their breast to their feet... On their heads

A Renaissance masterpiece – The
Crowning of the Elect *fresco
painted by Luca Signorelli
between 1499 and 1502 in the
Cappella di San Brizio in Orvieto
Cathedral. Signorelli based his
visions of heaven and hell on the
writings of Dante.*

they wore crowns intertwined with gold and roses and lilies and surrounded with pipes of most precious stones… Their garment emitted a very strong aroma, like perfume…'

As towns and cities began to develop throughout early medieval Europe, with all the public sanitation issues that entailed, it's difficult not to notice an emphasis on detailing the sweet smells and pure air that awaits in paradise, as well as the unimaginably luxurious building materials involved. For example, Pope Gregory I relates in his *Dialogues* the encouraging story of a soldier who returns from the brink of death to report the glimpses of heaven he caught:

Across the bridge, there were green and pleasant meadows carpeted with sweet flowers and herbs. In the fields groups of white-clothed people were seen. Such a sweet scent filled the air that it fed those who dwelt and walked there. The dwellings of the blessed were full of a great light. A house of amazing capacity was being constructed there, apparently out of golden bricks, but he could not find out for whom it might be.

The later encyclopedic 68-volume *Acta Sanctorum* (Acts of the Saints), chronicling the lives of the Christian saints, adds details to this picture with a hagiography of the reclusive nun called Gherardesca of Pisa, who received a vision of heaven as a city-state before her death in 1269: 'All the streets were of the purest gold and the most precious stones. An avenue was formed by golden trees whose branches were resplendent with gold. Their blossoms remained rich and luxuriant according to their kind, and they were more delightful and charming than anything we can see in earthly pleasure-gardens.'

Seven castles housing souls of the common people encircled the city, whom the city aristocracy would deign to visit three times a year. At the lowest level of the social order of heaven were less important fortresses, where the lower orders resided. (Here is a reflection of the urbanisation Sister Gherardesca was witnessing taking place outside her earthly window – it's estimated that between 1150 and 1250 the number of urban developments in central Europe rose from 200 to around 1500.)

Thomas Aquinas (1225-1274) tackled the inconsistencies of heaven with supreme scholastic intellectual precision. It is from Aquinas that we have the idea of heaven being an intercommunicating body of saints: 'Since all the faithful form one body, the good of each is communicated to the others…

FOLLOWING PAGES: Fishing for Souls *by Adriaen van de Venne, 1614. An allegorical painting made during the Twelve Years' Truce (1609-1621) between the Dutch Republic and Spain, showing the jealousy between the various religious denominations.*

We must therefore believe that there exists a communion of goods in the Church.' But he also took time to address more specific details of heaven, for example in his *Summa Theologiae* he is referring to Genesis when stating: 'Now animals and plants were made for the upkeep of human life... Therefore when man's animal life ceases, animals and plants should cease.'

Along with no plants and animals in the afterlife, he also thinks that the souls in heaven would be motionless, a desirable part of one's final coming to rest. The bodies of the blessed also had their own quality of light in paradise, he says, different to that of the angels and saints. He also writes of the view from heaven – specifically of the punishments suffered by the damned in hell, which was a common opinion at the time. The residents of heaven have no pity for these infernal souls; indeed, their punishment is part of the joy of the blessed, as God's justice is fulfilled. The later American theologian Jonathan Edwards (1703-1758) agreed – his biographer, Samuel Hopkins, writes in *The Life and Character of the Late Reverend Mr Jonathan Edwards* (1765) that if the fires of hell were extinguished it would 'in great measure obscure the light of heaven, and put an end to great part of the happiness and glory of the blessed and be an irreparable detriment to God's eternal kingdom'.

When it comes to descriptions that cement the image of heaven in the popular consciousness, there are two significant figures remaining to examine. Before we meet again with Emanuel Swedenborg, it is crucial to examine Dante's *Paradiso* and its lasting legacy, including Michelangelo Caetani's 1855 map, which so helpfully lays out the Dantean universe. As he had done previously for hell and purgatory, Dante took the vague, shining idea of heaven and formalised it with architecture; and yet it is a very different work in its details.

There is nothing comparable to the specific vignettes of the tortures afflicted on the damned – these are the consequences of their actions motivated by their choice of self. In *Paradiso*, ego of character is removed, for this is the Kingdom of God. The goal of the virtuous is not to endure experiences like their counterparts in the burning netherworld, but to expand in the love and concentration of God, to eventually ascend to understanding God and his will. The souls that Dante encounters in heaven are waiting, in a blissful state of divine love, to be joined by their physical bodies following the Resurrection.

Ascent of the Blessed *by Hieronymus Bosch, painted between 1505 and 1515. An angel guides a naked soul through a tunnel of light to heaven, where figures await their arrival. The angels below assist souls in their ascent to make the same passage.*

The heaven of the *Paradiso* is an inversion of Dante's descent into the terrible Inferno. Leaving behind the sphere of Earth, the poet ascends the sky, climbing the spheres of the Ptolemaic cosmos, in which each planet is believed to be embedded in the crystal shell of a set of enormous spheres, like transparent Russian nesting dolls, that spin and therefore account for the orbits of the planets. Dante encounters a succession of figures who grow more solid and brighter in form as he nears the very outer layer of the universe, the Empyrean, the dwelling of God.

The first sphere of the Moon, for example, is inhabited by fickle women who did not stick to one good course of life; then onward he travels to the spheres of Mercury, Venus, the Sun (home to the theologians, including Thomas Aquinas), Mars, Jupiter, Saturn, the fixed stars and the outermost sphere, the Primum Mobile, before the Empyrean. When God is sighted, He is a dazzling point of light at the centre of nine spinning circles, which turn out to be the nine choirs of angels. At every moment, the imagery is circular and spherical, in Dante's perfect synthesis of religious and scientific belief of his time. In 1861, Gustave Doré illustrated the story brilliantly, giving us one of the most stunning and enduring images of heaven (see page 213).[1]

As the science of astronomy developed in the seventeenth century, and no glimpse of heaven was caught in the lenses of increasingly powerful telescopes, the question became: if heaven was not to be found among or beyond the stars, then where could it be? One answer to this was that it did not exist in a location at all. The German Christian mystic Jakob Böhme (1575-1624) answered the question of where the soul goes after death by suggesting that heaven and hell are not places, but are within ourselves: 'There is no Necessity for it to go anywhere… The Soul has Heaven and Hell within itself already…There is no such kind of entering in; because Heaven and Hell are everywhere, and universally co-exist.'

Gerrard Winstanley (1609-1676), one of the founders of the Protestant radical group the True Levellers, or Diggers, which extolled an early form of communism, sneered at the idea of 'an outward heaven, which is a fancy your false teachers put into your heads to please you with while they pick your purses'.

---

1 When Gustave Doré's publisher refused to take the risk of publishing the illustrator's collection of 135 illustrations for Dante's *Divine Comedy* in 1861, Doré did it himself. In just two weeks the book had sold out, and he received a telegram from the same publisher: 'Success! Come quickly! I am an ass!'

FOLLOWING PAGES: The Fall of the Rebel Angels *(1562) by the Netherlandish Renaissance artist Pieter Bruegel the Elder. Lucifer tumbles to hell with his legion of fallen angels, as told in Revelation.*

William Bond, a member of another dissenting group called the Ranters, wrote in 1656 that 'there was neither heaven nor hell except in a man's conscience, for if he had a good fortune and did live well, that was heaven: and if he lived poor and miserable, that was hell, for then he would die like a cow or horse.' The English explorer Sir Walter Raleigh (c.1552-1618) reportedly denied the existence of heaven and hell entirely, declaring instead that 'we die like beasts and when we are gone there is no more remembrance of us.'

Such decrying made the vision-writings of Emanuel Swedenborg all the more impactful. Over his lifetime he wrote eighteen published works and revealed the sights of heaven as had been shown him, most vividly in his *Arcana Cœlestia* ('Heavenly Mysteries' or 'Secrets of Heaven'), 1749-1756. 'Let me tell about the things that arise directly out of the light', he writes. 'There are diamond-like atmospheres that flash in all their most minuscule elements, as if they were made of diamond pellets… There are atmospheres seemingly made of translucent pearls glowing from within… There are atmospheres afire with gold, it seems, or with silver, or with diamond-like gold and silver. There are atmospheres composed of multicoloured flowers so small they cannot be seen.' The gardens in heaven 'are breathtaking. Huge parks containing every kind of tree come into view, so beautiful and so charming that they defy all power of imagination. Absolutely everything appears in its loveliest springtime and its loveliest bloom, with stunning magnificence and variety.'

Swedenborg was also shown much of the architecture of heaven: 'In addition to cities and mansions, I was sometimes able to see decorative elements, such as those that appear on stairways and main doors. These elements moved as if they were alive, and changed with ever fresh beauty and symmetry.' He even toured the homes of angels (and claimed to have experience angelic eternal life for himself):

All angels have their own houses to live in – magnificent houses… They are so clear to see, so visible, that nothing could be more so. Houses on earth are almost nothing by comparison… The houses of good spirits and angelic spirits usually have porticoes, or long entryways, vaulted and sometimes doubled, where they walk. The walls of the walkways are formed in many different ways and are graced with flowers and flower garlands woven in an extraordinary manner.

OPPOSITE: *Gustave Doré's illustration of the Rosa Celestial of* Paradiso, *the third and final part of Dante's* Divine Comedy. *This is the Empyrean, the highest heaven, and dwelling place of God.*

FOLLOWING PAGES: *A 1783 print of the church as a ship, sailing away from the material world towards the City of God, with the different Catholic factions vying for control. Based on an allegorical painting of the French Wars of Religion that was confiscated from the Jesuit College in Billom in 1762 to be used as evidence against them during the dissolution of the Jesuit Order in France.*

Estampe, du Tableau trouvé dans l'Eglise, des ci-devant

isans-JÉSUITES de Billom en Auvergne. 2.ᵉ n 1762.

His is a romantic heaven, a mirror image of Earth, where at the highest celestial heaven the Garden of Eden is restored and angels wander naked, 'because nakedness corresponds to innocence'.

Such are the centuries of layered images that form the bedrock of the modern popular image of heaven, a concept still colourfully evolving. In July 1999, Pope John Paul II publicly declared that heaven is not a place filled with angels and harps on fluffy clouds, but rather 'a state of being' following death. 'The heaven in which we will find ourselves is neither an abstraction nor a physical place among the clouds', he told pilgrims in St Peter's Square. It is, he said, 'a living and personal relationship with the Holy Trinity... Close communion and full intimacy with God... heaven is a blessed community of those who remained faithful to Jesus Christ in their lifetimes, and are now at one with His glory.'

Shortly after these remarks, Father Gino Concetti, chief theologian at *l'Osservatore Romano*, suggested that there could still be messages dispatched from heaven to Earth: 'Communication is possible', he writes, 'between those who live on this earth and those who live in a state of eternal repose... it may even be that God lets our loved ones send us messages to guide us at certain moments in our life.'

ABOVE LEFT: *A psychic portrait of Christ.* ABOVE RIGHT: *Another scene of heaven, by Georgiana Houghton (1814-1884), a British artist and spiritualist medium. She began producing her 'spirit drawings' in 1859 during private seances, with her hand guided by the souls of the dead. In 1871, Houghton gave a disastrous exhibition of her work to a baffled London public, which nearly bankrupted her.*

And what of the future of heaven? In 1961, the year of Yuri Gagarin's *Vostok 1* shuttle mission, an official Vatican spokesman, swept up in the public fascination of the space race, excitedly suggested that astronauts might encounter angels on other planets. Some fifty years later, in a 2012 interview with *US Catholic*, Vatican astronomer and Jesuit Brother Guy Consolmagno proposed that the prospect of intelligent life elsewhere in the universe could be theologically fruitful. 'If we ever find intelligent life', he suggests, 'we will have an interesting dialogue about the nature of the incarnation.'

The afterlife, as channelled through a spirit guide and painted as an assurance of life after death. From A Goodly Company *(1933) by Ethel le Rossignol, who served as a nurse during the First World War (for which she was awarded the British War Medal and the Victory Medal) before becoming a medium in 1920.*

MAPPING THE GARDEN OF EDEN

In the Welsh language there is a particularly beautiful word: hiraeth. It has no direct English translation, but the general sense of the term is an overwhelming feeling of grief and longing for one's people and land of the past, a kind of amplified spiritual homesickness for a place one has never been to. This word came to mind when collecting together maps drawn over the centuries by Europeans attempting to give a specific earthly location for an unearthly concept: the Garden of Eden. For it is one of the most ancient and alluring of all myths: man's first and perfect home, lost and lying somewhere out there over the seas, waiting to be rediscovered; a terrestrial microcosm of a heavenly realm in some desert oasis or on a remote island in the distant east.

A late map of the Garden of Eden by Pierre Mortier, 1700, based on the theories of Pierre Daniel Huet, Bishop of Avranches. Its caption reads: 'Map of the location of the terrestrial paradise, and of the country inhabited by the patriarchs, laid out for the good understanding of sacred history, by M. Pierre Daniel Huet.'

The Garden of Eden *by Lucas Cranach for* Biblia, Das Ist: Die Gantze Heilige Schrifft Deudsch *(1530), Martin Luther's German translation of the Bible.*

Many took its existence to be literal. When Christopher Columbus made his third voyage of discovery (1498-1500), it was with a stated goal of searching for the Earthly Paradise. Though it may well have been a way to charm the Catholic monarchs who sponsored his expeditions, when he discovered the Orinoco River he declared that he had discovered one of the four rivers of Eden. Encountering the local people, he sang in praise of their natural innocence and took it as a sign, he wrote, that he had reached proximity with heaven – though this did little to prevent him from plundering the region's wealth.

The Garden of Eden was where God 'drove out the man; and he placed at the east of the Garden of Eden Cherubims, and a flaming sword which turned every way, to keep the way of the tree of life' (Genesis 3:24). Eden is described as the source of four giant rivers: the Pishon, the Gihon (Nile), the Hiddekel (Tigris) and the Phirat (the Euphrates). (This has similarities to the legend of Mount Meru in Jainism, Hinduism and Buddhism, which is believed to be man's ancient home, the seat of gods and a place where four rivers burst forth into the cosmic ocean.)

FOLLOWING PAGES: *Hieronymus Bosch's magnificent triptych* The Garden of Earthly Delights *(c.1490-1505). The Garden of Eden is depicted on the left panel, the Last Judgement on the right, while in the centre is a paradise panorama of naked figures and fantastical creatures.*

The account in Genesis left biblical commentators puzzled, however – had Adam and Eve's garden really existed on Earth? If so, where and could it still be found? Centuries of obsession locating and mapping the Earthly Paradise in Latin Christian Europe was largely triggered in the fifth century by St Augustine's literal interpretation of scripture, which had divine authority – the events recorded in the Bible were God's communication with mankind. And so it was understood that the Garden of Eden was a specific place on Earth.

The essential imagery of a four-rivered garden somewhere in the farthest east is how one finds the story's earliest graphic form on maps. On the medieval *mappae mundi*, which are usually oriented with east as north, Jesus is found at the top, presiding over a paradoxical combination of legend and geography. The example presented opposite is the *Map Psalter*, so called because it was discovered in a book of psalms. Though relatively small in size, it is one of the great medieval maps of the world (though probably not the original, more likely a copy of a work long since lost that once hung in the Westminster Palace bedchamber of Henry III around the mid-1230s). Just like the famous *Hereford Mappa Mundi*,

The Garden of Eden with the Fall of Man *by the master-pairing of Jan Brueghel the Elder and Pieter Paul Rubens,* c.1615.

The Map Psalter *created in London c.1262-1300, depicting Adam and Eve just below Jesus at the head of the map. Jerusalem is at the centre, the British Isles to the lower left.*

its detail provides insight into contemporary understanding of ancient history, scripture and geography. One of these vignettes is a painting of the Eden tale – the portraits of Adam and Eve sit just below Jesus, atop their four rivers.

In 1406, a Byzantine manuscript of Ptolemy's *Geographia*, generally thought to have been lost to Western Europe until this time, was sent from Constantinople to Venice and, after the publication of Jacopo Angelo's translation of the second-century work into Latin, it began to have a profound effect on European cartography. The development of sea charts had already introduced out of necessity the practical purpose – and therefore scientific approach – of mapping, moving away from the historical display of *mappae mundi*. But it was in the fifteenth century that the east-oriented layout of the *mappae mundi* popularly gave way to a preference for the Ptolemaic model, the basis of modern mapping, with the introduction of a mathematical system using global coordinates, and the establishment of north at the head of the map.

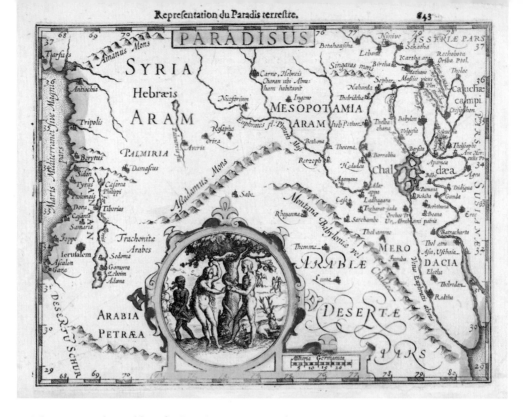

Athanasius Kircher's Topographia paradise terristris…, *a map of the Earthly Paradise described in Genesis, c.1675.*

This presented a problem for Renaissance map-makers – belief features, such as the Earthly Paradise, had no place on maps that prized accuracy over religious decoration – and so the garden began to be dropped from maps, its abandonment a symbol of the progression in contemporary thinking as the sixteenth century dawned. Consequently, attempts were made to rationalise the myth: scholars such as Joachim Vadian (1484-1551) and Johannes Goropius Becanus (1519-1573) argue that the garden could be interpreted not as a specific tangible territory, but as Adam and Eve's pure and blissful existence before the arrival of sin. Martin Luther (1483-1546) found it pointless to argue about the exact location of the garden, as it was likely destroyed with everything else in the Great Flood, a victim of Man's sin.

The French theologian John Calvin (1509-1564) agreed with the idea that the garden had been drowned and lost, but presented the comforting theory that God maintained affection for Man and had left remnants of the paradise on Earth. Calvin accompanied his *Commentary on Genesis* (1553) with a map of Mesopotamia with its rivers, and claimed the garden to have once been in the region. He interpreted the 'four rivers' to mean four 'heads' of rivers, that is, two channels carrying the water to the garden, and two bearing it away, and showed how this could fit the Mesopotamian system. Calvin's idea was

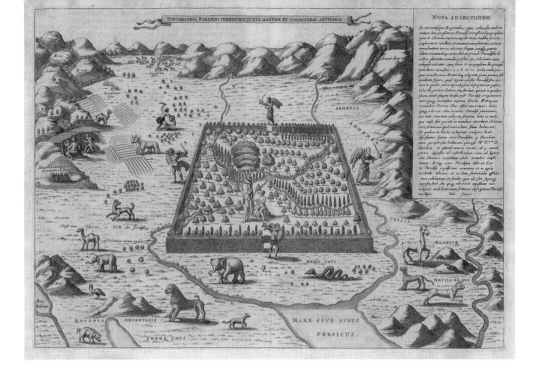

adopted and developed by various sixteenth-century publishers of the Bible, some of whom clarified the idea for their readers and also went a step farther, drawing the site of the Fall on the map. In 1607, Gerardus Mercator and Jodocus Hondius developed this design with greater geographic detail for the map *Paradisus*, which is dominated by a vignette of Adam and Eve below the apple tree.

Map from 1607 by Mercator and Hondius showing Paradise near Babylon.

The four-river design of the garden was dropped from maps soon after. One of the last to feature the emblem was Sir Walter Raleigh, who, a few years after Hondius, included the Earthly Paradise on his map of 'Arabia the Happie', together with a scattering of other biblical imagery. The idea that the Garden had been obliterated by the Flood continued to be accepted, but from this point there was a shift in theory as to its original location: attention turned from Mesopotamia to Armenia, which, at this time, included the region between the Upper Euphrates and Lake Urmia, the Black Sea and the Syrian desert.

Perhaps, it was thought, the biblical River Pishon was, in fact, the River Phasis, and the Gihon the River Araxes. After this, the Holy Land was offered as another alternative, but this was more to do with dogmatic convenience than any geographic indication. By the eighteenth century, the cartography of the Earthly Paradise was, for most, a decoration of antiquity, and it was left to its perennial verdancy in imagination and religious myth.

THOMAS MORE'S *UTOPIA*

Having spent time wandering through heavenly and earthly paradises, it felt logical to conclude with a few explorations of that related, more modern idyll: the utopia. The word was invented by Sir Thomas More (1478-1535) as the setting and title of his 1516 book, deriving it from the Greek prefix *ou-* (not) and *topos* (place). So 'utopia' literally means 'nowhere'.

More was an English lawyer, humanist, statesman and Catholic martyr, who was both knighted by King Henry VIII in 1521, and canonised by Pope Pius XI in 1935. Born into a wealthy merchant family, through his writings he was the figurehead of a lively intellectual scene in sixteenth-century London, out of which grew the early manifestations of humanism.

Utopia is his most famous work, depicting a society of a fictional island, a pagan and communist city-state, with detailed accounts of its religious, political and social customs in detail – a paradise essentially defined as the opposite of sixteenth-century London. Though it's now referred to simply as the *Utopia*, the original title of the 1516 work that introduced the utopian concept, and proved a hit among its target readership of humanists and elite public officials, is a little longer: *A truly golden little book, no less beneficial than entertaining, of a republic's best state and of the new island Utopia.*

The point of *Utopia*, like all fantasy worlds and alternative universes in this genre of More's invention, is to satirise and embarrass the society of its time, a model to modify attitudes and perhaps even qualify conduct. The book was a radical starburst of an idea in 1516. The utopian city's every municipal feature is a denunciation of More's own London. Despite (or perhaps because of) the fact that More himself was a lawyer, no one of that profession exists in utopian society.

More was also at one point Lord High Chancellor of England for Henry VIII, yet in the book rails quite extraordinarily against private ownership of property in favour of shared ownership, damning capitalist social order as a 'conspiracy of the rich', orchestrated by men who are 'greedy, unscrupulous and useless'. He denounces the nobleman who lives off the labour of the poor, and the landlord who evicts tenants as 'one insatiable glutton and accursed plague of his native land'. Utopians are the *agricolae* (cultivators) of their land, rather than the *domini* (proprietors). All share in the fruits of this farming.

OPPOSITE: *A woodcut by Ambrosius Holbein, illustrating a 1518 edition of Sir Thomas More's* Utopia. *In the lower left, Raphael describes the island Utopia.*

The Utopian alphabet from More's Utopia

In Utopia, monarchs should pledge to have no more than 1000lb (450kg) of gold at any one time – in fact, the value of precious metals is scorned; gold and silver are used to make simple things like chamber pots and shackles. One lively episode in the book concerns the visit of the Anemolian ambassadors, who attempt to impress their hosts by dressing in gold clothes, chains, rings and jewels, only to find that the Utopians think of them as slaves or fools for doing so.

In Utopia, 'though no one owns anything, everyone is rich'. War is for animals, and armies should be dissolved. The Utopians spend as much time as possible cultivating their minds, too, providing the source of true happiness. All citizens must work a useful trade, but only for six hours a day; and 'men and women alike' must spend the rest of the time on intellectual betterment. Brothels and drinking dens

The only surviving example of Ortelius's map of a More-inspired utopia – only twelve copies were originally printed.

were not to be found. At the same time, life was not a bed of roses in utopia. On certain feast days, wives threw themselves at the feet of their husbands, confessing to some lapse in domestic duty. Adultery was punished with enslavement. Men were allowed to see their future wife naked before agreeing to marriage – though women were accorded the same entitlement. Suicide is condemned, but euthanasia allowed.

Among the topics discussed by More in *Utopia* are penology, state-controlled education, religious pluralism, divorce, euthanasia and women's rights. As a demonstration of his learning, wit and imagination, the book helped elevate More's status to one of Europe's foremost humanists, as *Utopia* was translated across the continent, the progenitor of a new literary genre. As well as the illustrations of the island and language of the Utopians, one of the rarest associated artistic treasures is a map by the great Dutch cartographer Abraham Ortelius (1527-1598), who was so inspired by More's book that he produced a chart of utopia, of which only twelve copies were printed, and of those only one survives today (see above).

THE EDIBLE PARADISE
OF COCKAIGNE

For medieval Europeans in search of a more sensual paradise
than the church could offer, Christian heaven had stiff
competition in the form of a realm that catered (literally) to
every gluttonous whim, an extensively described utopian realm
known the Land of Cockaigne (sometimes 'Cockagne'). This
fantasy paradise gripped the public's waking and sleeping
imagination for centuries and, though little known about
today, is recorded in tens of thousands of texts of mythical and
satirical writings of the period.

*Pieter Bruegel the Elder's 1567
critical depiction of Cockaigne
and its residents highlights the
spiritual emptiness of indulging
in the deadly sins of gluttony
and sloth.*

The allure was in its simple concept: it was an upside-down world, where the rules of reality were reversed. Dreamworlds tell us about the realities of their dreamers – in this instance, the fantasy offered was for all the social and institutional hierarchies, all the drudgeries and hardships of daily life, to be turned upside down in this land of plenty. At the same time, it was an inversion of the religious idea of paradise.

Sinful gluttony and idleness are not just encouraged, but are foundational to Cockaigne life. There, work is forbidden. Houses are made of food; roasted pigs wander around offering cutlery to help one carve them up; cooked geese fly themselves into hungry mouths; and grilled fish leap from the rivers and fall at one's feet. Dream denizens are showered with cheeses, sweetmeats and buttered larks that rain down from the sky; the trees are made of butter; monks can beat their abbots; nuns happily show their bottoms; and everyone is paid to sleep. The weather is always pleasant; the wine pours endlessly; and everyone stays young for eternity.

A 1725 map of the 'Schlaraffenland' (the German equivalent of Cockaigne), by the German cartographer Johann Homann. Each vice has its own kingdom – e.g. Pigritaria (Land of Indolence), Lurconia (Land of Gluttony) and Bibonia (Land of Drink).

The origin of the word Cockaigne is debated, but most agree that the word seems to derive from a word meaning 'cake'. One of the earliest references is made in an Irish text *Aislinge Meic Conglinne* (The Vision of MacConglinne), written in the late eleventh century, a parody of the standard saint's vision. In this story, a king possessed by a ravenous gluttony demon is cured by a vision of the impossibly gluttonous Cockaigne. The Germans call the place Das Schlaraffenland, the Italians Il Paese della Cuccagna and the Dutch legend of Het Luilekkerland (literally, the lazy-luscious-land) originates with the idea. The Spanish have their equivalent, País de Cucaña, while the Swedish have Lubberland, derived from the word *lubber* (a fat lazy fellow). The last was popularised in a 1685 broadside ballad:

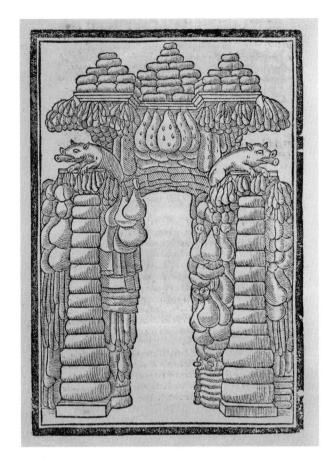

A grand arch made of food that was erected on 23 June 1629 in Via della Porta del Caputo in Naples, as part of the annual celebrations of Duke Antonio Álvarez de Toledo, Viceroy of Naples. Fireworks burst out of the mouths of the pigs at the top.

There is a ship, we understand,
Now riding in the river;
'Tis newly come from Lubberland,
The like I think was never;
You that a lazy life do love.
I'd have you now go over,
They say the land is not above
Two thousand leagues from Dover.

J. Deacon, An Invitation to Lubberland

By the end of the Middle Ages, belief in the dream of Cockaigne had faded and it was appropriated for moral purposes as a cautionary tale against gluttony; but there are residual traces of the idea to be found in later history.

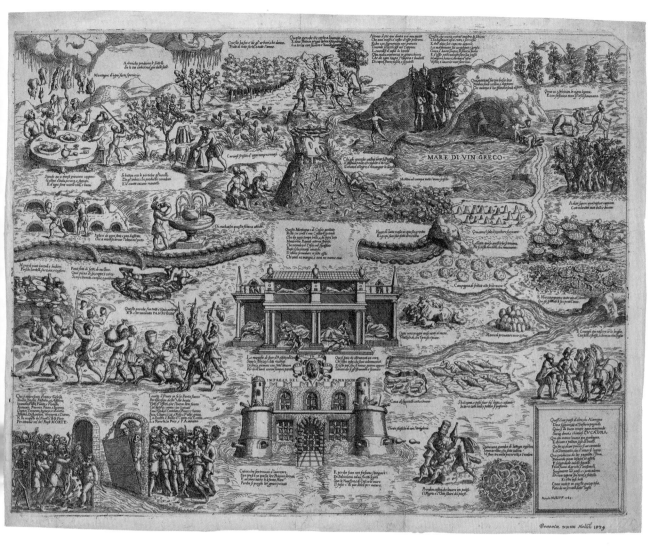

The Land of Cockaigne
by Niccolò Nelli, 1564.

In Edwardian Britain, Cockaigne was used as a moralist metaphor for greed and drunkenness, and adopted by the rest of country as a nickname for London. (This was memorialised by the composer Edward Elgar with his 1900 concert overture *Cockaigne (In London Town), Op. 40.*)

There is also a Neapolitan tradition that survives today known as the 'Cockaigne tree', a pole that is usually greased and fixed with a prize like a cooked ham at its top, for the person who manages to climb it. Much crueller than this, though, was its Cockaigne-inspired forbear, a tradition that took place in the sixteenth to eighteenth centuries known as the 'edible monument'. To bring the dreamland and its buildings made of food to life, at festivals and royal celebrations great

Cuccagna posta sulla Piazza del Real Palazzo

A. Casino coperto di Lardo, Panzette, Prosciutti; · Balanstri di Cacio Cavallo . · · Capre, Palombi, e Galline . D. Due stili sopra de quali due Vsti : E. Fontana di vino . m. Prosciutti, Cacio Cavallo, M. Parte della Chiesa di
Cacio cotto vecchio Cavalle, e Vino, Sopressate; B. Monte con tre strade coperto di Cacio Ca · C. Peschiera con Papere, ed Anatre, n da Fordune, uno da teme, e l'altr F. Fontana d'acqua, genere, Prosciutti, e Pane es altro di diversa qualità. S. Fran.co di Paola
Galline, Papere, Galli d'India, e Palombi, con vallo, e Cacio di Moca, Pecore, Bovi, Porci con varie sorti di Pesce da Denna tutti guarniti d'Oro. G. Botte di Vino. l. Piedestali, e Vasi composti di Pa · L. Lazzari che corrono a dare il Sacco · N. Spevieria di S.Spirito .
XI

structures were built out of piles of breads, cheeses and meat
and dessert buffets. In Italy, this was known as a *cuccagna*, and
was a favourite entertainment of the aristocracy.

The image shown here, titled *Cuccagna posta sulla Piazza
del Real Palazzo* by the engraver Giuseppe Vasi, shows one
such Cockaigne palace built in 1747 in front of the Palace of
Naples in celebration of the birth of King Carlo's son Filippo.
Every inch of the structure is laden with food: bacon, pancetta
and prosciutto, aged *caciocavallo* cheese, bread and *sopresatta*
sausage, live hens, geese, ring-doves, with more cheese
carpeting the paths up the hill and the balustrades. In the
centre is a fountain of wine. The two tall poles in the centre are
greased *cuccagna* trees with suits of fine clothing attached to the
top for whomever succeeds in the climb. The entertainment for

The Cuccagna *(Cockaigne)
monument commissioned by
Charles III, erected in front of
the royal palace in Naples on
16 November 1747, in celebration
of the birth of the king's first-born
son Filippo. Peasants were
allowed to rush into the edible
garden and devour the food, for
the entertainment of the watching
royal family.*

the gathered elite came in watching the spectacle of the crowd of starving commoners (visible on the sides of the image) being released into the grounds to gorge on and fight over the food, and snatch as much as they could carry for later. Sometimes, fireworks were let off as an added effect.

The dream of Cockaigne may have long since faded, but there is, in a sense, a way of travelling to at least the shadow of the myth. The names of two Dutch villages of Kockengen (in Utrecht) and Koekange (in the province of Drenth), both derive from the word Cockaigne – this was a shrewd manoeuvre by residents in around the fourteenth century, to lure workers to the otherwise unexciting area to help cultivate the peat bogs.

Description of the Land of Cockaigne, 1606, showing rainfalls of diamonds and pearls (top left); and cooked meat (top right).

An extraordinary allegorical map of the 'Island of Felicity', 1743, thought to be by Johann Martin Weis. The map was made for l'Ordre de la Félicité, a quasi-Masonic secret society established in France in the early 1740s. The Island of Felicity features the fortified castle of Perfect Happiness, and sits south of the Wild Sea and north of the Favourable Sea. Avoid the Rocks of Caprice, the Banks of Temptation and the Rocks of Prudery and one can anchor at the ports of Wealth, Beauty, Complaisance, Virtue, Equality and of course Felicity, each with a route to the castle of Perfect Happiness. Be careful not to stray from the Road of Talents, to become lost in the Swamp of Pleasures.

DOWIE'S ZION

When choosing the final location to be described in this book, I thought it worth featuring a place that one can actually visit, should one be curious enough. Certainly, it can be said of the American city of Zion, born of an attempt at creating a real utopia, that it has the power to inspire sufficient curiosity. Today, 40 miles (64km) north of Chicago, can be found the city wholly designed and constructed by John Alexander Dowie (1847-1907), an Edinburgh-born faith healer, self-proclaimed reincarnated prophet and suspected arsonist.

Dowie had first moved with his parents from Scotland to Australia in 1860, where he was ordained as a pastor in 1872. Ten years later, he was operating his own ministry out of a theatre, enrapturing a small following of Sydneysiders with his claims of miraculous healing powers. Moving to Melbourne in the 1880s, he had the funds to build his own tabernacle and to embark on an international preaching tour, finding great success in the US, in San Francisco and Chicago.

In 1888, his Melbourne church burnt down in suspicious circumstances – the insurance, by good fortune, allowed him to pay off huge debts, and he fled to America. By now, Dowie had taken to wearing magnificent coloured robes and proclaiming himself the spiritual return of the biblical prophet Elijah 'the

ABOVE: *John Alexander Dowie, faith healer and founder of the city of Zion, in his robes as Elijah the Restorer.*

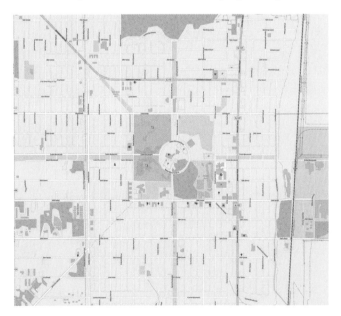

LEFT: *The City of Zion as it appears today. Dowie's Union Jack-inspired design remains discernible.*

Restorer'. He charged huge tithes for the gift of his healing power. All publicised attempts to prove him a charlatan and shut down his operation simply amplified his fame.

By 1901, Dowie's success with his Christian Catholic Apostolic Church was so great that he was able to secretly purchase 6000 acres (2428 hectares) of real estate some 40 miles (64km) north of Chicago to found his own city, Zion, as a new home for himself and his 6000 followers. Zion is one of the few cities in the world to have been completely planned out before construction; even more unusual is the design itself – Dowie laid out the entire city in the form of the Union Jack flag, as a nod to his origins. The street names were all taken from the Bible – existing roads include: Damascus, Deborah, Ebenezer, Elim, Elijah, Elisha, Emmaus, Enoch, and Galilee Avenue; all bordered by Bethlehem Avenue running east to west on the north side.

Zion was entirely owned by Dowie, but settlers were offered 1100-year leases (100 years to usher in the new Kingdom of Christ, and 1000 years to enjoy Christ's millennial reign. Then, presumably, one had to renew). Dowie ruled his utopia with an iron-bound rulebook – almost every enjoyable feature of daily life of the outside world was banned – this included gambling, dancing, baseball and football, swearing, spitting, theatres, circuses, alcohol, tobacco, pool, pork, oysters, medicine and doctors, politicians and, for some reason, tan-coloured shoes.

Zion police officers each carried a billy club in one holster and a Bible in another, and their helmets were painted with a dove and the word PATIENCE. At the height of his powers, Dowie had a personal wealth of several million dollars and 50,000 followers worldwide. 'The one incomprehensible element in the man's gigantic success is the personal luxury in which he lives, and his superb refusal at the same time to account for any of the sums of money entrusted to him', wrote the Irish MP and journalist T. P. O'Connor, who was baffled by Dowie's success:

His horses are worth a fortune in themselves; his carriages are emblazoned with armorial bearings; his wife is said to dress with the gorgeous extravagance of an empress. When he travels, hemmed round with a little army of servants, the prophet of humility and self-denial has a special train chartered, and whenever the spiritual burdens become too great a tax there is a delightful country residence belonging to him in which to retreat from the clamour and importunate appeals of the faithful.

Dowie had these colourful pamphlets printed and distributed to advertise the pleasures of life in his paradise city.

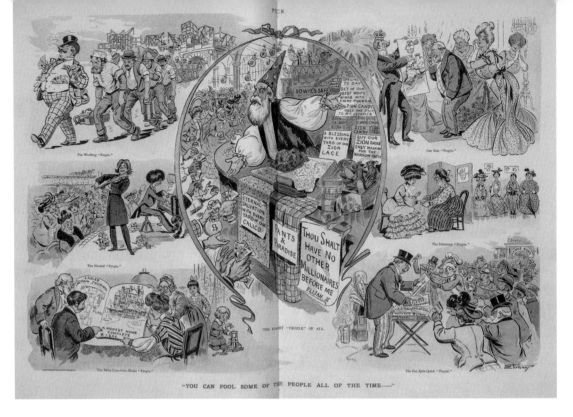

A satirical cartoon from the publication Puck, *14 October 1903, of John Alexander Dowie at its centre, dressed as a wizard offering salvation and other products to gullible customers.*

In 1905, Dowie suffered a stroke and travelled to Mexico to recuperate. In his absence he was deposed by a lieutenant, Wilbur Glenn Voliva, who discovered that Dowie had embezzled around $3 million of Zion public funds. Dowie died in 1907, and was buried in Zion's Lake Mound Cemetery; but, quite fantastically, the story of Zion doesn't end there.

Though Voliva made no claims to prophethood or mystical healing, he possessed equally colourful eccentricities. He set about trying to rescue Zion from bankruptcy with even stricter control over the city's running, even dictating who married whom. Anyone who dared to smoke a cigarette in Zion was branded a 'stinkpot' – in fact, Voliva erected the world's first anti-smoking billboards in Zion in 1915. His most cherished belief, however, which he promoted passionately and enshrined into Zion's religious code, was that the idea of the 'globe' was a lie, that scripture could be clearly interpreted as stating that the Earth was flat. In 1914, he offered a widely publicised reward of $5000 to anyone who could prove otherwise – a prize he never paid out.

The citizens of Zion would eventually learn that they were in no better position under Voliva's leadership than that of Dowie. In 1927, it was discovered that Voliva had embezzled even greater amounts of municipal funds than his predecessor, amassing a personal wealth of $5 million. Governance went

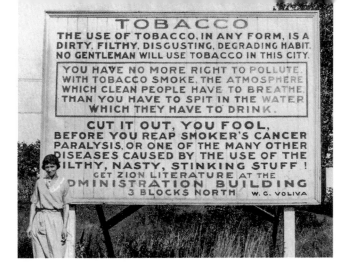

to the people, who immediately voted for a compulsory city car sticker featuring a spherical globe as a logo that Voliva was forced to display. Despite having claimed he would live to 120 due to his diet of Brazil nuts and buttermilk, Voliva died in 1942 after a tearful confession of his embezzling and other misdeeds. Today, Zion has a population of about 25,000, and is the site of a planned baseball stadium for the Fielders team, owned by the actor Kevin Costner. Earthly paradise, we are reminded, and its simple luxuriance of purity, has always eluded its pursuers – even when they have attempted to construct it for themselves.

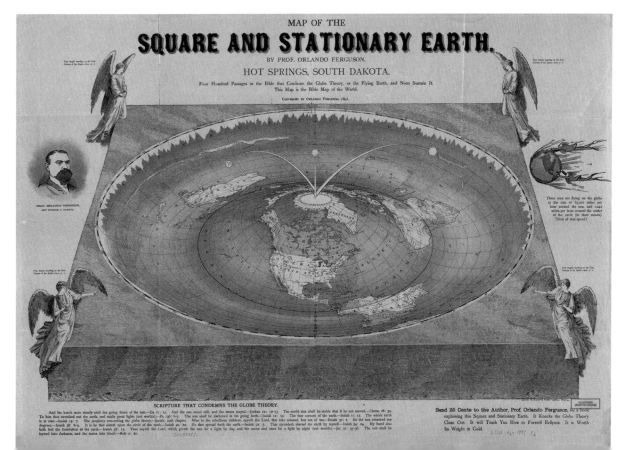

CONCLUSION

How best to end a book about the End? For Dante, chief architect of afterworld construction, the journey of *The Divine Comedy* was of course always on a heading of one destination. In the final canto, the poet finally reaches God, who is in the form of three circles of light:

In the deep and bright essence of that exalted Light, three circles appeared to me; they had three different colours, but all of them were of the same dimension; one circle seemed reflected by the second, as rainbow is by rainbow, and the third seemed fire breathed equally by those two circles.

Inside these dazzling circles, Dante can just make out the figure of Christ, and he is bathed in their light as he attempts to comprehend the humanity and divinity of the Holy Trinity. As the realisation comes, in a sweeping wave of understanding that even he finds impossible to articulate, his soul is enveloped and absorbed into God's love, resulting in one of the most beautiful parting lines in all of literature:

But already my desire and my will were being turned like a wheel, all at one speed, by the Love which moves the sun and the other stars.

There is also, I would suggest, as much poetry to be found in the acceptance of the impenetrable veil of the mystery. To me, one of the most beautiful expressions of this notion can be found in the *Ecclesiastical History of the English People* (731) of the Venerable Bede, as he relates the deliberations of King Edwin of Northumbria conducted in 627 over accepting the Christian faith. In contribution to the debate, one of his men compares mortal life to the flight of a sparrow passing through a lighted hall, as outside rage storms of rain and snow: 'The sparrow, flying in at one door and immediately out at another, while he is within, is safe from the wintry tempest, but after a short space of fair weather, he immediately vanishes out of your sight, passing from winter to winter again. So this life of man appears for a little while, but of what is to follow or what went before we know nothing at all.'

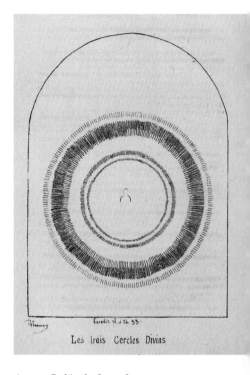

ABOVE: *God in the form of three circles of light, encountered by Dante at the end of his* Divine Comedy. *From an 1846 edition of the poem illustrated by John Flaxman.*

OPPOSITE: The Dance of Death, *commissioned by the order of Observant Franciscans (Order of Friars Minor) for a church sacristy in the seventeenth century as a reminder of mortality.*

FOLLOWING PAGES: The Temptation of St Anthony *by Pierre Picault, after Jacques Callot (c.1729). St. Anthony is dragged from his cave (lower-right) while Satan fills the sky.*

SELECT BIBLIOGRAPHY

Abbott, D. P. (1907) *Behind the Scenes with the Mediums*, London: Kegan Paul & Co.

Albinus, L. (2000) *The House of Hades: Studies in Ancient Greek Eschatology*, Aarhus: Aarhus University Press

Almond, P. C. (2016) *Afterlife: A History of Life After Death*, London: I. B. Tauris & Co.

Almond, P. C. (1994) *Heaven and Hell in Enlightenment England*, Cambridge: Cambridge University Press

Barrett, Sir W. (1917) *On the Threshold of the Unseen*, London: Kegan Paul & Co.

Beard, M. (ed.) & Rose, J. (ed.) & Shotwell, S. (ed.) (2011) *A Swedenborg Sampler*, West Chester: Swedenborg Foundation

Brandon, S. G. F. (1967) *The Judgment of the Dead*, London: Weidenfeld & Nicolson

Brown, P. (2015) *The Ransom of the Soul: Afterlife and Wealth in Early Western Christianity*, London: Harvard University Press

Bruce, S. G. (2018) *The Penguin Book of Hell*, New York: Penguin Books

Budge, E. A. W. (1975) *Egyptian Religion: Ideas of the Afterlife in Ancient Egypt*, London: Routledge & Kegan Paul

Budge, E. A. W. (1905) *Egyptian Heaven and Hell*, La Salle: Open Court Publishing

Burnet, T. (1739) *Hell's torments not eternal*, London

Casey, J. (2009) *After Lives: A Guide to Heaven, Hell, & Purgatory*, Oxford: Oxford University Press

Cavendish, R. (1977) *Visions of Heaven and Hell*, London: Orbis Publishing

Chadwick, H. (1966) *Early Christian Thought and the Classical Tradition*, Oxford: Clarendon

Clark, T. J. (2018) *Heaven on Earth: Painting and the Life to Come*, London: Thames & Hudson

Copp, P. (2018) *The Body Incantatory: Spells and the Ritual Imagination in Medieval Chinese Buddhism*, New York: Columbia University Press

Dalley, S. (trans.) (1989) *Myths from Mesopotamia: Creation, The Flood, Gilgamesh and Others*, Oxford: Oxford University Press

Dawes, Sir W. (1707) *The Greatness of Hell-Torments. A sermon preach'd before King William, at Hampton-Court*, London: H. Hills

Delumeau, J. (1995) *History of Paradise: The Garden of Eden in Myth & Tradition*, New York: Continuum

Ebenstein, J. (2017) *Death: A Graveside Companion*, London: Thames & Hudson

Eco, U. (2013) *The Book of Legendary Lands*, London: MacLehose Press

Ehrman, B. D. (2020) *Heaven and Hell: A History of the Afterlife*, London: Oneworld

Gardiner, E. (2013) *Egyptian Hell: Visions, Tours and Descriptions of the Infernal Otherworld*, New York: Italica Press

Gardiner, E. (2013) *Hindu Hell: Visions, Tours and Descriptions of the Infernal Otherworld*, New York: Italica Press

Gardiner, E. (1989) *Visions of Heaven & Hell Before Dante*, New York: Italica Press

Gearing, W. (1673) *A Prospect of Heaven; or, a treatise of the happiness of the Saints in Glory*, London: T. Passenger and B. Hurlock

Gordon, B. (ed.) & Marshall, P. (ed.) (2008) *The Place of the Dead: Death and Remembrance in Late Medieval and Early Modern Europe*, Cambridge: Cambridge University Press

Guggenheim, W. & Guggenheim, J. (1995) *Hello from Heaven!*, New York: Bantam Books

Hall, W. J. (1843) *The Doctrine of Purgatory and the Practice of Praying for the Dead*, London: Henry Wix

Hartcliffe, J. (1685) *A Discourse Against Purgatory*, London

Hornung, E. (1999) *The Ancient Egyptian Books of the Afterlife*, Ithaca: Cornell University Press

Johansen, M. (2015) *The Geography of Heaven*, Monroe: Electric Tactics

Kajitani, R. & Kyosai K. & Nishida, N. (2017) *Hell in Japanese Art*, Tokyo: PIE International

Kroonenberg, S. (2011) *Why Hell Stinks of Sulphur: Mythology and Geology of the Underworld*, London: Reaktion Books

Law, B. C. (2004) *Heaven and Hell in Buddhist Perspective*, New Delhi: Pilgrims Publishing

Le Goff, J. (1981) *The Birth of Purgatory*, Chicago: University of Chicago Press

Levin, H. (1972) *The Myth of the Golden Age in the Renaissance*, Oxford: Oxford University Press

Lipner, J. (2019) https://www.bl.uk / sacred-texts / articles / the-hindu-sacred-image-and-its-iconography

Lucian, (trans.) A. M. Harmon *Works of Lucian* (1913), London: Loeb

MacGregor, G. (1992) *Images of Afterlife: Beliefs from Antiquity to Modern Times*, New York: Paragon House

Markos, L. (2013) *Heaven and Hell: Visions of the Afterlife in the Western Poetic Tradition*, Eugene: Cascade Books

Mercer, S. A. B. (1949) *The Religion of Ancient Egypt*, London: Luzac

Messadié, G. (1996) *A History of the Devil*, New York: Kodansha

Mirabello, M. L. (2016) *A Traveler's Guide to the Afterlife*, Rochester: Inner Traditions

Oldridge, D. (2012) *The Devil: A Very Short Introduction*, Oxford: Oxford University Press

Paparoni, D. (2019) *The Art of the Devil: An Illustrated History*, Paris: Cernunnos

Pleij, H. & Webb, D. (trans.) (2001) *Dreaming of Cockaigne: Medieval Fantasies of the Perfect Life*, New York: Columbia University Press

Russell, J. B. (1997) *A History of Heaven: The Singing Silence*, Princeton: Princeton University Press

Scafi, A. (2013) *Maps of Paradise*, London: British Library

Schall, J. V. (2020) *The Politics of Heaven and Hell: Christian Themes from Classical, Medieval, and Modern Political Philosophy*, San Francisco: Ignatius Press

Spufford, F. (ed.) (1989) *The Vintage Book of the Devil*, London: Vintage

Stanford, P. (2002) *Heaven: A Traveller's Guide to the Undiscovered Country*, London: HarperCollins

Stanford, P. (1998) *The Devil: A Biography*, London: Arrow Books

Thigpem, P. (2019) *Saints Who Saw Hell: And Other Catholic Witnesses to the Fate of the Damned*, Charlotte: Tan Books

Took, J. (2020) *Dante*, Princeton: Princeton University Press

Turner, A. (1993) *The History of Hell*, New York: Harcourt Brace & Co.

Wiese, W. (2006) *23 Minutes in Hell: One Man's Story about What He Saw, Heard, and Felt in that Place of Torment*, Lake Mary: Charisma House

Zaleski, C. G. (1987) *Otherworld Journeys: Accounts of Near-Death Experience in Medieval and Modern Times*, Oxford: Oxford University Press

INDEX

Page numbers in *italics*
refer to illustrations

A'aninin people 148
A'aru 20, 22, 149, 150-3
'Abbas I, Shah *185*
Abraham 61, 132, 138
Abu Hurairah 188
Abu Sa'id Gurkan, Sultan *184*
Abzu 26
Acheron, River 52, 89, *91,*
    106, 107
Achilles 50
Acta Sanctorum 205
Adam 201, 222, 223, *223,*
    224, 225
Adrian V, Pope *145*
Aeacus 54, 170
Ægir 57
Aeneas *50, 51,* 52
Agüeros, Father Pedro
    Gonzalez de *15*
Ahl al-Kisa 132, 133
Ahriman 31
Ahura Mazda 29, 31
Airavata *158,* 159
Aislinge Meic Conglinne 232
al-Firdaws 187
Alcyonian Lake 51
Alexander the Great 31
All Souls, Oxford University 144
Allah 11, 63, *132, 133,* 185, 188
Álvarez de Toledo, Duke
    Antonio *232*
Amaravati 158-9
Ambrose, St 201
Amish *129*
Amitābha 163, 166, *166*
Ammit 22, *23,* 151
Anastasius II, Pope *106, 107*
Andhataamistra 36
Andrewes, Lancelot 200
ángel arcabucero 182
Angel Heart 103
Angelico, Fra 98, *202*
Angelo, Jacopo 223
Angrbooda 57
Ani 20-2, *20*
Anthony, St. *244-5*

Antichrist 10, 92, *103, 196*
Anubis 21-2, *23,* 151
Anvār-i Suhaylī 189
Apep 92-3
Apocalypse of Paul 84
Apocalypse of Peter 84, 88
Apocrypha 84
Aprathisth 36
Aquinas, Thomas 205, 208, 209
Al-A'raf, Surah 62-3
Arali 26
Ardā Wīrāz *30-1,* 31
Arikha, Abba 196
Arjuna *158*
As-Sirāt 30, 60, 184
Ashurbanipal, King 27
Asphodel Fields (Meadows) 52,
    134, 170
Atharvaveda 34
Atrahasis 25
Augustine, St 16, 88, 136, 143,
    194, 202-3
Augustus II *18-19*
Avernus, Lake 52
Averroes 138
Avesta 29, 30
Avici 44
Avitus of Vienne 136
Ayyad, Qadi 61-2, 63
Azrael 60
Aztec *70, 71,* 72-3, *72,* 176, 180

ba *20*
Ba'al 76
Babylonians 93
Bael *14*
Baldr *57,* 190
Baldrs Draumar 59
bardo 133
Bardo Thodol 133-4, *135*
Barzakh 60, 132-3
Basilica Sant' Apollinare
    Nuovo *96,* 97
Becanus, Johannes Goropius 224
Bede, Venerable 88, 144, 242
Bedford, Duke and Duchess of *4*
Bedford Hours 4
Beelzebub 92
Behaim, Martin 146

Bellini, Giovanni *142*
Benedict XVI, Pope 147
Benedict of Nursia 201-2
Benivieni, Girolamo 106
Bermejo, Bartolomé *137*
Berry, Duke of *85*
Berthold of Regensburg 14
Bhagavad Gita 159
Bhagavata Purana 14-15, 35-6,
    155, 161
Bhavacakra *42*
Bible 142, 144-5, 149, 222,
    225, 239
    Biblical heaven 14, 194-217
    Biblical hell 74-131
Big Sand 148
Blake, William *80, 81, 95,*
    147, 199
Bloemaert, Cornelis *54*
Böhme, Jakob 209
Bolognini, Bartolomeo *110-11*
Bond, William 213
Book of Ardā Wīrāz 9, 10, *30-1,* 31
Book of the Dead 20-2, *20, 23,*
    151, 200
The Book Pertaining to Paradise,
    Its Description, Its Bounties,
    and its Intimates 186
Bosch, Hieronymus *50,* 74,
    97-8, 117, *138, 208, 220-1*
Botticelli, Sandro 112, *114-15*
Bourdaloue, Louis 117, 120
Brahma 11, 14, 155, *156-7,* 158,
    159, *160,* 161
Brahman 38-9, 154
Brahmanda Purana 155
Brahmapura 161
Briareus 52
Brückner, Max *190*
Bruegel, Pieter the Elder *210-*
    11, 230
Brueghel, Jan the Elder *222*
Brueghel, Jan the Younger *50*
Buddha 40, 45, 46, 133, 134, 163
Buddhism 32, 38, 40-6, 133, 158,
    162, 163-6, 219
Budge, E. A. Wallis 22-3, 153
Bundahišn 30, 31
Buraq 65, *66-7*

Burgesse, Michael *125*
burial urns *174*
Burnet, Thomas 11, 14

Caesar, Julius 138
Caetani, Michelangelo *112-13*,
    113, *143, 203*, 208
Callot, Jacques *244-5*
Calvin, John 224-5
Camposanto Monumentale 97
Canaanites 76
Cape Matapan 18, 51
Capet, Hugh *145*
Carlo, King *233*, 234
Carthusians *201*
Caso, Alfonso *179, 180*
Catholicism 116, 132, 141-7,
    182, 183, 194, *214-15*, 216-17
    see also Christianity
caves 148
Ceiba tree 174
Cerberus 51, 52, 54, 59, 105, 170
Chandogya Upanishad 38-9
Charon *51*, 52, *52-3*, 54, *106,
    107*, 170, *170*
Chateaubriand, François-René
    de 143
Chichimecas 180
Chichiualquauitl 73
Chicomoztoc 176
Chimera 52
Ch'in Shih Huang-ti,
    Emperor *167*
Chinese mythology 18, 46-8, *167*
Ching-tu (Pure Land) school 163
Chinvat bridge 29-30, *29*, 89
Christianity 29, 35, 56, 57, 59,
    62, 149, 188
    Garden of Eden *4*, 15, 92,
        147, 168, 186, 216, 218-25
    limbo 136-9
    purgatory 141-7
    see also Bible
Chü-lu-ts'ui-lüeh 41
Church of New Jerusalem 128
Cipactli 180
Cizin 69, 72
Clement of Alexandria 138
Cochin, Nicolas 8-9, *195*
Cockaigne 189, 230-7
Cocytus 52
Codex Borgia *70, 71*
Coffin Texts 151

Colombe, Jean *146*
Columbus, Christopher 219
*Compendium of Demonology
    and Magic 101*
Concetti, Father Gino 216
Consolmagno, Brother Guy 217
Constantine I 200
Coppo di Marcovaldo *104*
Craesbeeck, Joos van *12-13*
Cranach, Lucas *168*, 219
cuccagna 234, 234-5
Cuneiform tablets *27*
Cusco School *182*
Cyprian 201
Cythera *173*

da Modena, Giovanni *110-11*
Dādestān i denig 30, 31, 132
Damasus, Pope 96
Dante Alighieri *100, 145*,
    147, 204
    Divine Comedy 146-7, *203*,
        242, *242*
    Inferno 15, 18, *19*, 98-9,
        104-15, 116, 138-9, 209
    Paradiso 208-9, *212*
Daoism 162-3
Davidson, H. R. Ellis 56
Davies, Arthur B. *171*
Day of Judgement 60, 61, 78, 84
Death *6*, 80, *116*
Defoe, Daniel 92, *93*, 99
della Quercia, Priamo *106, 107*
Demmerlé, Marguerite 141
demonic floats *18-19*
demons 14
*Descent of Inanna into the
    Underworld* 27
Devi Bhagavata Purana 36
Devil 27, 79, *85*, 91, 92-103,
    128, 202
devil trap bowls *27*
Dictionnaire infernal 14, *14*
Dionysus 51
Diyu 46-8
Domitian 79
Dong Yue Miao temple *45*, 46
Doré, Gustave *139, 209, 212*
Dowie, John Alexander 238-41
Drexel, Jeremias 116-17, 120-1
drinking cup *70*
Duat 20-3, 151, *203-4*
Dumuzid 27

Dunton, John 201
Dürer, Albrecht 17, 97-8

Earthly Paradise 15, 147, *147*,
    219, 222, 224, *224*, 225
East: heavens of the 162-7
    hells of the 40-6
Eastern Orthodox Church
    138, 147
Edwards, Jonathan 208
Egyptians 20-3, 25, 92-3,
    149, 150-3
Ehecatl 180
Ehrman, Bart D. 78
einherjar 190, 192
Electra 138
Elgar, Edward 233
Elijah the Restorer *238*, 238-41
Elliot, T. S. 113
Elysian Fields (Elysium) 52,
    134, 169-72
Empyrean 209, *212*
Enki 25
Epic of Gilgamesh 25
Epic Literature 35
Ereshkigal 27
Ersetu 26
Escalante, Tadeo *128*
Eurydice 51
Eustathius of Thessalonica
    170-1
Eve 222, 223, *223*, 224, 225
Eyck, Jan van *116*

Father of Lies 92
Faunus 93
Fengdu 18, 46
Fenrir 57, 193, *193*
Ferguson, Professor
    Orlando *241*
Fields of Mourning 52, 170
Fields of Rushes 20, 22, 149, *150*
Flaxman, John *242*
Florentine Academy 107
Florentine Codex 73
Flower Mountain 176
Folkvang 57
Fortune, Reo F. 148
Foscolo, Ugo *144*
Francken, Frans the Young *124*
Freyja 57
Furniss, John 128-9
Fursey 88

Gabriel 65
Galilei, Galileo 107-8
Galle, Cornelis the Elder *100*
Garbhodaka Ocean 36
Garden of Eden *4*, 15, 92, *147*,
    168, 186, 216, 218-25
Gathas 29
Gaulli, Giovanni Battista *122*
Geefs, Guillaume *102*
Gehenna 61, 74-83, 144
Genesis 95, 186, 201, 208, 219,
    222, 224, *224*
Genshin 45
Gherardesca of Pisa 205
Geryon 52
Gesù *122*
Gey-Hinnom 61
al-Ghazali 61
Giotto 98
God 14, 63, 78, 84, 88, 94, 97,
    105, 116, 117, 122, 125, 131
    Divine Comedy 242, *242*
    Garden of Eden 219, 224
    heaven 194, 196, 198-9, 200,
        200, 201, 203, 208, 216
    limbo 136
    Lucifer and 96
    purgatory 144
Golden Age 168-9
Goltzius, Hendrick 97-8
Gorgons 52
Greek mythology 18, 50-4, 59,
    74, 93, 134, 168-73, *200*
Gregory I, Pope 88, 136,
    144, 205
Gregory of Tours 88
Grímnismál 57, 59
Gua *21*
Gugalanna 27

Hades 18, 50-5, 59, 74, 78, 80,
    134, 136-7, 169-70
Hadiths 10, 62, 63, 185, 187, 188
Halakhah 194
Hall of Ma'at 21, 151
Hamistagan 30, 31, 132
hana pacha 71, 178-9
harpies 52
Hatshepsut, Queen *152*, 153
heavens 148-241
Hebrews 74, 78, 94
Hector 138
Heede, Jean-Luc van den 8

Heiðrún 192, 193
Heimdallr *59*
Hekla 18
Hel 56-9, 190
Hel (goddess) 57, *57*
Hell, Livingston County 8, 9
Hell of the Flaming Rooster
    40-1
hell money 48
hell-mouth 90-1
The Hell Scroll 40-1
hells and underworlds 15, 18-
    131, 148
Helreið Brynhildar 59
Helvegr *59*
Henry III 222
Henry VI *4*
Henry VIII 227
Hercules 18, 51
Hermóðr 57, *59*
Hesiod 168, 169
Hildegard of Bingen 200, 204-5
Hinduism 11, 14, 32-9, 40-1,
    154-61, 219
Hiranyakaśhipu 34
Holbein, Ambrosius *226*
Holkham Bible Picture Book
    98, *194*
Hollar, Wenceslaus *141*, 146
Homann, Johann *231*
Homer 50, 53-4, 134, 170,
    171, 172
Hondius, Jodocus 225, *225*
Hopkins, Samuel 208
Horus *23*
Houghton, Georgiana *216*
*The Hours of Catherine of
    Cleves 90*
House of Lies 28-31
House of Song 28-31
Hsien-chiu-hu 41
Huet, Pierre Daniel *218*
Hunefer *23*
Huracán 175
Hussite manuscript *99*
Hydra 51

Ibn al-Qayyim 133
Ibn Arabi 133
Iceland 18, 58
Iineferti 150
Ilhuicatl-Meztli 180-1
Ilhuicatl-Omeyocan 183

Ilhuicatl-Tonatiuh 183
Illapa 179
Inanna 27, *27*
Inca 71-2, 178-80
incense burners *174*
India 32-9, 40-6, 154-61, *165*
Indra 32, 158, *158*, 159
infernal cartography 15, 105-15
International Theological
    Commission 139
Inti 179
Iran 29
Irenaeus, St 199
iri-gal 26
Irkalla 26
Ishtar *24*, 27
Islam 10, 11, 29, 30, 60-7, 92,
    132-3, 184-9, 200
Islamic Book of the Dead 187,
    188-9
Island of Felicity *236-7*
Islands of the Blessed 172-3
Israelites 74, 78
Itihasa 32
Ixion *54*
Ixtab 176

Jade Emperor 46, *48*
Jahannam 60-7, 184, 188
Jainism 32, 38, *38*, *39*, 158, 219
James VI, King 14
Jannah 60, 184-9
Japan 46, *166*
Jelling Runestone *192*
Jena Codex *99*
Jerome, St 96, 136
Jerusalem, new 80, *129*, 149,
    197-8, *197*, 200, *223*
Jesus Christ 35, 54, 61, *74*, 77,
    78, 80, 84, *94*, 95, 96, *96*, 97,
    105, 131, *192*, 242
    heaven 196, 199, 200, 202,
        216, *216*
    limbo 136-7, 138, *139*
    mappae mundi 222, 223, *223*
Jibril *187*
Jnana Bagi 161
Job 94
John, St 196, 197, 198, *199*
John of Patmos 79
John Paul II, Pope 136, *147*, 216
Jörmungandr *191*
Jou't, Victor 140-1

Joyce, James 121
Judaism 29, 74-8, 92, 94, 141, 194, 196
Judas Maccabeus 142
Judgement Day 84, 132, 149
Julian, St 89
Julian of Toledo 88

ka 21
Kalasutra 43
Kalmsikta 36
Kennedy, John F. *48*
Kerberos 52
K'iché 72
Kigal 26
Kimhi, Rabbi David 76
King James Bible 78
Kingdom of Osiris 20
Kinich Ahau *174*
Kircher, Athanasius *224*
Krishna *159*
Kronos 168, 169, 173
Kukku 26
Kumbhakarṇa *156-7*
K'unlun, Mount 162-3
Kur 24-7, 74

Lacandon 69, 72
Lactantius 200
Land of Cockaigne 230-7
Landino, Cristoforo 106
Last Judgement *220-1*
Lattimore, Richard 54-5
Lazarus 137
Le Goff, Jacques 142, 144, 147
le Rossignol, Ethel *217*
Leo XIII, Pope 128
León-Portilla, Miguel 73
Lernaean Hydra 52
Lethe 52, *172*
Liber Floridus 197
Liber Scalae Machometi 189
lilitu 93
limbo 132, 134, 136-9
Limbo of the Infants 136
Limbo of the Patriarchs 136
Limbourg brothers *85*
linen balls *151*
Litovchenko, Alexander *170*
lokas 155
Loki 57, 59
los Ríos, Pedro de 73
Lubberland 232

Lucifer 89, 92, *94*, 96-7, 98, *100*, *102*, 105, *195*, *210-11*
Lugentes Campi 52
Lund, Johann *78*
Luther, Martin 224

Maalik 65, *65*
Mahabharata 14, 35, *158*
Mahadevi 14
Maharaurava 36, 43
Mahavastu 45-6
Majjhima Nikaya 46
Mama Killa 179
mandala *163, 166*
Manetti, Antonio 106, 107, *108, 109*, 112
Mantegna, Andrea *139*
Manus 148
Manuščihr 31
Manushchihr 132
mappae mundi 222-3
Map Psalter 222-3, *223*
Marcus, Brother 88-9
Markandeya Purana 36
Marmion, Simon *91*
Matsya *36*
Maya 68-71, 174-8, 183
Me'rāj-nāmas 61
Medici, Lorenzo di Pierfrancesco de' 112
Memling, Hans *118-19*
Menna 20
Mēnōg-ī Khrad 30
Mephistopheles 92, 102
Mercator, Gerardus 225, *225*
Mercury *171*
Meru, Mount 14, *154*, 158, *165*, 219
Mesoamerica: heavens 174-83
underworlds 68-73
Mesopotamia 24-7, 74, *92*, 224, 225
Metropolitan Master *70*
Metz, Gossuin de *109*
Mewar Ramayana 155, *156-7*
Meztli 180
Michael, archangel *75, 91*, 124, *196*
Michelangelo *77*
Mictlān *70*, 72-3, 180, 183
Mictlantecutli 72-3, *72*
Midgard Serpent 57, *191*
Midworlds 132-5

Milton, John 102, 124, *125*
Minos, King 170
Mishnah 194
Mithra 30
Moche civilisation *73*
moksha 38, 154
Moll, Rob 131
Moloch 76, *78*, 92
money, hell *48*
More, Thomas 226-9
Mortier, Pierre *218*
Moses 61
Mount Purgatory 147, *147*
muan bird 68, 69
Muhammad, Prophet 61, 62, 64, 65, *65*, *66-7*, *184*, 185-6, *186*, 188
Mulian Saves His Mother from Hell 48
Munkar 60
Museo delle Anime del Purgatorio 140-1, *140*

Nahj al-Faradis 184
Nahua 176, *178*, 180, 183
Nakir 60
Naraka 35, 41, 43-4, *48*
Narasimha *34*
Natali, Hieronymo 76
Native Americans 148
Necromanteion of Ephyra 18
Nelli, Niccolò *233*
Nergal 27
The Neville of Hornby Hours 200
Ngaju Dayak 148
Niflheim *56*
nirvana 163, 166
Norse mythology 56-9, 190-3
Nyingma school 133

Observant Franciscans *243*
Oceanus 50
O'Connor, T. P. 239
Odin *57*, 59, *59*, 190, 192, *192*, 193, *193*
Odysseus 50, 53
Ōjōyōshū 45
Olam Ha-Ba 194
Omecihuatl 183
Ometecuhtli 183
One Death 69, 72
Oriental Orthodox Church 147
Orpheus 18, 51, 138

Orphic tablets 55
Ortelius, Abraham 229, *229*
Osiris 20, 21, *23*, 151, 153, 200
Ovid 168-9

Padma Purana 36-8
Padmasambhava 133
Pakal, K'inich Janaab' *68*, 176
Palace of King Sargon II *25*
Pan 93, 98
Pandemonium 125
Panjtan 132, 133
paradises 148-241
Parvati *154*
Patala *33*, 36, 155
Patinir, Joachim *52-3*
Patrick, St 145
Paul, St 16, 84, 194, 196
Pausanias 51
Pazuzu *92*
P'eng-lai *167*
Perier, Alexandre *3, 126, 127*
Persian chainmail shirt *132, 133*
Peter, St 84, 95
Phlegethon 52
Picault, Pierre *244-5*
Pinamonti, Giovanni 121-2
Pindar 173
Pius XI, Pope 227
Plancy, Jacques Collin de 14, *14*
Plato 168
Plutarch 172
Pluto *51*
Pope, Alexander 134
Popol Vuh 69, 70, 174, 175
Pratapana 43
Prince of Darkness 92
Prose Edda 57, *57*, 58, *59*,
     192, 193
Protestantism 116, 122, 142,
     144-5, 209
Ptolemy 223
Puck 240
Pullen, Robert 143
Puranas 32, 35-6, 155, 161
Pure Land 163, 166, *166*
purgatory 132, 134, 140-7
Pyramid Texts 22, 23, 150-1

Queen of the Night *24*
Quetzalcoatl 72-3, *72*, *177*, *181*
Qur'an 10, 60, 61, 62-4, 133,
     184-5, 186, 187, 188

Ra 93
Ragnarök 57, 59, 193
Raleigh, Sir Walter 213, 225
Rama *155*
Ramayana 35, *155*, *156-7*
Ramesses IV *23*
Rán 57
the Ranters 213
Rastelli, Palmira 141
Raurava 36, 43
Rāvaṇa 35, *156-7*
Raziel 14
Revelation 14, 79-80, *82-3*, 97,
     196-8, *199*, 200, *210-11*, *241*
Rigveda 32, 34
The Roads to Heaven and Hell 130
Rodin, Auguste 18, *19*
Rök runestone *193*
The Roll of the New Fire 177
Roman Catholic Church 92,
     136, 138, 139
Romans 52, 54-5, 79, 93, 168-73
Rooster Angel of Prayer *187*
Rubens, Peter Paul *75*, *222*

Sachi *158*
Saehrimnir 192
Sahagún, Bernardino de 181
St John Climacus *198*
St Patrick's Purgatory *141*, 145-6
St Peter and St Paul's church
     10, *86-7*
Saladin 138
Saliba, Antonio de *123*
Samghata 43
Samjiva 43
saṃsāra 32, 154
Śaṅkhāsura 36
Santa Maria delle Anime del
     Purgatorio ad Arco 140
Saošyant 31
Sapa Inca 179
Sarasvati 159, *160*
Satan 15, 18, 62, 79, 91, 92,
     94-5, 98-9, 102, *102*, *104*,
     105, 124-5, 147, *244-5*
Satya-loka 155, 159, 161
Saundarya Lahari 14
Sauvage, Raymond 193
scarabs 20
Schlaraffenland *231*, 232
Scot, Michael 14
Scylla 52

Seerah 64-5
Sefer Raziel HaMalakh 14
Segal, Alan 74
Selden Roll 177
Semele 51
Seneca, Lucius Annaeus 54
Senenmut *152*
Sennedjem *150*
Sentient Beings *165*
Seven Death 69, 72
Seven Sins *51*
Shaalmali 36
Shamash 26
Shaw, George Bernard 54
Sheol 74-83, 136, 141
Shi, Master *29*
Shi'a *132, 133*
Shiva *154*
Siddhārtha Gautama 40
Sidraṭ al-Muntāhā 188
Signorelli, Luca *120*, *204*
Silos Apocalypse *82-3*
Simurgh 188
Sisyphus 54
skalds 56
Sleipnir *59*
Sohrevardi 188
Spina, Alphonsus de 14
Square Temple, Tell Asmar *26*
Stanhope, John Roddam
     Spencer *172*
Statius *145*
Stothard, Thomas 102, *102*
Sturluson, Snorri 59, *59*, 190, 193
Styx 52, *52-3*, 170, *170*
Sufism 133
Sukhavati (the Pure Land) 163,
     166, *166*
Sunniulf, Abbot of Randau 88
Supay 71, 72
Sutherland, John 131
Sutra on the Eighteen Hells 41
sutras 45
Svarga-loka 36, 155, 158-9, *158*
Swabhojan 36
Swanenburg, Jacob Van *51*
Swedenborg, Emanuel 127-8,
     208, 213, 216
Swinden, Tobias 15, 120-1, *121*

Taamistra 36
Taima Mandala *166*
Tamoanchan 73

Tanakh 74-8
Tantalus 54
Taoism 46, 162-3
Tapana 43
Ta'rikh al-Hind al-Gharbi 64
Tartaruchus 84, 88
Tartarus 52, 78, 121, *121*, 134, 170
Taube, Karl *179*
Tempesta, Antonio *169*
Temple, Sir Richard Carnac *165*
Temple of the Inscriptions, Palenque *68*, 69
Teotihuacan Spider Woman *179*
Teramo, Jacobus de *94*
Teti *23*
Thai manuscripts *49*
Thaloques 181
Thirteen Heavens 180
The Thirty-Seven Nats 48, *165*
Thor 193
Thurkill 89
Thutmose III 153
Tibetan Book of the Dead 133-4, *135*
Tibetan hell texts 46
Tintoretto *148-9*
Tiresias 53
al-Tirmidhi 185-6
Tityos 54
Tjängvide image stone *192*
Tlahuiztlampa *181*
Tlaloc *73*, *179*, 180, *180*, 181
Tlālōcān *73*, 176, *179*, 181, 183
Tlaltícpac 180
Tlazolteolt 180
Toltecs 180
Tomb of the Diver *173*
Tomb of Wirkak *29*
Tonatiuh 183
Topheth 76
totenpass 55
Traini, Francesco *97*
Très Riches Heures *85*
True Levellers 209
tsagli 44
Tu-i-nan-ch'ieh 41
Ṭūbā 63, 188
tumi 73, *176*
Tundal 88-9, *91*
Twain, Mark 102
The Twilight Zone 103
The Two *177*

ukhu pacha 71, 178
Underworld Painter 55
underworlds 18-131, 148, 151, 153, 169-70
Urban II, Pope 204
ushabti 20, 21, *23*, 151
utopias 148-241
Utopia 226-229

Vadian, Joachim 224
Vaikuntha 14
Vaitarani River 35
Vajrabhairava *164*
Valgrind 192
Valhalla 57, 58, 190-3
Valkyries 190, 192
valley of Hinnom 76-7, 79
Vamana Purana 36
Vamoth *193*
Van Gogh, Vincent 8
Van Impe, Dr Jack 15
Vasi, Giuseppe *233*, 234
Vedas 32, 161
Venne, Adriaen van de *206-7*
Venus *173*
Vercelli Book 91
Vidēvdād 30
Vikings 56-9, 190-3
Virgil 52, 104, 105, *106*, *107*, 138, *145*, 147, 171
Virgilius *100*
Virgin Mary 183
Vishnu 14, *33*, *34*, 36, 161
Vishnu Purana 36
vishvarupa 159
Vishwakarma, Lord 159
Visio Tnugdali 88-9
The Vision of Thurkill 89
The Vision of Tundal 91
volcanoes 18, 148
Voliva, Wilbur Glenn 240-1, *241*
Völuspá 59
Vulgate Bible 96, 97

Wak-Wak 63, *64*
Watteau, Jean-Antoine *173*
We-ilu 25
Weis, Johann Martin *236-7*
Wheaton, Henry *56*
Whiston, William *125*
Wiese, Bill 131
William of Auvergne 143-4
Winchester Psalter *91*

Winstanley, Gerrard 209
The World of Things Obvious to the Senses 16
Wrinkle Face *73*

Xibalba 69, 70, 175
Xiwangmu 163
Xōchipilli *71*
xrafstars 31

Yama 35, 36-7, *37*, 38, *42*, 46
Yasna 29
Yggdrasil *58*, 59
Yudhishthira, King 35

zabibatan 63
Zaganti, Maria 141
Zaqqum 63-4, 188
Zarathustra 9, 10, 29, *30-1*, 31
Zeus 54, *54*, 168, 169, 173
Zhuangzi 163
Zion 238-41, *238*
Zoroastrians 9, 10, 28-31, 62, 78, 132

ACKNOWLEDGEMENTS

I would like to express my deep appreciation to all who provided such indispensable help in the creation of this book: to Charlie Campbell at CCLA, to Ian Marshall at Simon & Schuster, and Laura Nickoll and Keith Williams for their tireless work in creating such a beautiful book. Thank you to Franklin Brooke-Hitching for enduring years of questions, and to my entire family for their support. Thanks also to Alex and Alexi Anstey, Jason Hazely, Daisy Laramy-Binks, Megan Rosenbloom, Lindsey Fitzharris, Matt, Gemma and Charlie Troughton, Georgie Hallett and Thea Lees, and to my friends at *QI:* John, Sarah and Coco Lloyd, Piers Fletcher, James Harkin, Alex Bell, Alice Campbell Davies, Jack Chambers, Anne Miller, Andrew Hunter Murray, Anna Ptaszynski, James Rawson, Dan Schreiber, Mike Turner and Sandi Toksvig.

I am especially grateful to those who have been so generous in lending expertise and allowing the reproduction of the magnificent images collected here, in particular: Daniel Crouch and Nick Trimming at Daniel Crouch Rare Books and Maps, Richard Fattorini at Sotheby's, the staff of Boston Rare Maps, Southampton, Mass., USA, and HS Rare Books, Buenos Aires, Argentina. Thanks also to the wonderful staff of the British Library, the Metropolitan Museum of Art, the Library of Congress, the New York Public Library, the Wellcome Collection and the John Carter Brown Library.

PICTURE CREDITS

PP1, 58 Norman B. Leventhal Map Center; P3 John Carter Brown Library; P4 British Library; P6 The Society of Antiquaries of London; INTRODUCTION; P9 Princeton University Library; P11 (both images) Biblioteca Nacional de España/Wikipedia.co.uk; PP12-13 State Art Gallery, Karlsruhe; P14 (both images) Library of Congress; P15 Seville University Library; P16 Boston Public Library; P17 Houghton Library, Harvard University; PART ONE: HELLS AND UNDERWORLDS; PP18-19 (background image) Heidelberg University Library; P19 Jahuey, Wikipedia.co.uk; P20 (top) © The Trustees of the British Museum; PP20-21 Keith Schengili-Roberts; P21 (top) Werner Forman / Universal Images Group / Getty Images; P22 Rama, Wikipedia.co.uk; P23 (top) © The Trustees of the British Museum; P23 (bottom) Chipdawes, Wikipedia.co.uk; P24 BabelStone, Wikipedia.co.uk; P25 Jastrow, Wikipedia.co.uk; P26 Rosemaniakos; P27 (both images) Marie-Lan Nguyen; P28 Edward Brooke-Hitching; P29 Smithsonian; PP30-31 (all images) Princeton University Library; P33 Victoria and Albert Museum, London; P34 British Library; P36 British Library; P37 Los Angeles County Museum of Art; P39 Anishshah19, Wikipedia.co.uk; PP40-41 Nara National Museum (public domain); P42 Wellcome Library; P44 Himalayan Art Resource; P45 Michael Gunther, commons.wikimedia.org; P47 Wellcome Collection; P48 (left) New York Public Library; P48 (right) Edward Brooke-Hitching; P49 Wellcome Library; P50 Metropolitan Museum of Art; P51 Museum De Lakenhal, Leiden; PP52-53 Museo Nacional del Prado; P54 Rijksmuseum; P55 (top) Remi Mathis; P55 (bottom) The J. Paul Getty Museum, Villa Collection, Malibu, California; gift of Lenore Barozzi; P56 British Library; P57 Robarts Library, University of Toronto; P59 (top) Royal Danish Library; P59 (bottom) National and University Library of Iceland; P60 Christie's; P62 Free Library of Philadelphia; P64 Metropolitan Museum of Art; P65 The David Collection, Copenhagen / Pernille Klemp / Wikipedia.co.uk; PP66-67 National Museum of India; P68 Ark in Time, flickr.com; P69 Museum of Fine Art Houston (Public domain); P70 (top) Public domain; P70 (bottom) Metropolitan Museum of Art; P71 Public domain; P72 (left) Public domain; P72 (right) Heritage Image Partnership Ltd / Alamy Stock Photo; P73 (top) Museo Larco, Lima, Perú. ML0044199; P73 (bottom) Metropolitan Museum of Art; P74 Metropolitan Museum of Art; P75 Yorck Project; P76 Cornell University Library; P77 Courtesy of the Vatican Museums; P78 Heidelberg University; P80 Brooklyn Museum; P81 National Gallery of Art, Washington; PP82-83 British Library; P85 Condé Museum; PP86-87 Edward Brooke-Hitching; P90 The Pierpont Morgan Library © Photo SCALA, Florence; P91 (top) J. Paul Getty Museum; P91 (bottom) British Library; P92 PHGCOM, Wikipedia.co.uk; P93 British Library; P94 The Warburg Institute; P95 Yorck Project; P96 Public domain; P97 Luca Aless; P98 British Library; P99 Národní museum; P100 Rijksmuseum; P101 Wellcome Collection; P102 (top) Cantor Arts Center, Stanford University; P102 (bottom) Luc Viatour; P103 (left) Library of Congress; P103 (right) Edward Brooke-Hitching; P104 Public domain; PP106-107 (all images) British Library; P108 Cornell University Library; P109 (top) British Library; P109 (bottom) Cornell University Library; PP112-113 (all images) Cornell University Library; PP114-115 Vatican Library; P116 Metropolitan Museum of Art; P117 Wellcome Library; PP118-119 National Museum, Gdańsk; P120 Yorck Project; P121 University of California Libraries; P122 LivioAndronico, Wikipedia.co.uk; P123 Daniel Crouch Rare Books; P124 Credit unknown; P125 (top) Barry Lawrence Ruderman Antique Maps; P125 (bottom) Beinecke Library; PP126-127 (all images) John Carter Brown Library; P128 Jeremyboer, Wikipedia.co.uk; P130 Library of Congress; PART TWO: LIMBO, PURGATORY AND OTHER MIDWORLDS; PP132-133 (chainmail) Metropolitan Museum of Art; PP132-133 (background image) Indianapolis Museum of Art; P135 Nyingma Lineage; P137 Museu Nacional d'Art de Catalunya; P138 Indianapolis Museum of Art; P139 (bottom) Frick Museum, NYC / Barbara Piasecka Johnson Collection; P141 Thomas Fisher Rare Book Library; P142 Yorck Project; P143 Cornell University Library; P145 British Library; P146 Condé Museum; P147 Yorck Project; PART THREE: HEAVENS, PARADISES AND UTOPIAS; PP148-149 Sonia Chaoui; P150 Metropolitan Museum of Art; P151 Bristol Culture / Bristol Museum & Art Gallery; P152 Metropolitan Museum of Art; P154 Victoria and Albert Museum, London; P155 British Library; PP156-157 British Library; P158 (top) Los Angeles County Museum of Art; P158 (bottom) Robarts Library, University of Toronto; P159 Arthur M. Sackler Gallery, National Museum of Asian Art; P160 British Library; P161 Wellcome Library; P162 (both images) Library of Congress; P163 Rubin Museum of Art, Gift of Shelley and Donald Rubin, C2006.66.509 (HAR 977); P164 Metropolitan Museum of Art; P165 (both images) New York Public Library; P166 Metropolitan Museum of Art; P168 National Museum of Norway; P169 Rijksmuseum; P171 (top) Phillips Collection; P171 (bottom) © Alfredo Dagli Orti/Shutterstock; P173 (top) Collection of the Royal Academy of Painting and Sculpture; P173 (bottom) Michael Johanning; PP174-175 (all images) Walters Art Museum; P176 Metropolitan Museum of Art; P177 The Bodleian Libraries, University of Oxford, MS. Arch. Selden. A. 72 (3); P179 Thomas Aleto; P180 Teseum, Wikipedia.co.uk; P181 FAMSI; P183 Mestremendo, Wikipedia.co.uk; P184 Illustrated double folio from the 'Nahj al-Faradis', commissioned by Sultan Abu Sa'id Gurkan, Timurid Herat, c.1465 (opaque pigment & gold on paper), Islamic School, (15th century) / Private Collection / Photo © Christie's Images / Bridgeman Images; P185 Walters Art Museum; PP186-187 David Collection; P189 Walters Art Museum; P190 De Agostini Editore/agefotostock; P191 Árni Magnússon Institute, Iceland; P192 (top) Berig, Wikipedia.co.uk; P192 (bottom) National Museum of Denmark; P193 (top) NTNU University Museum CC BY-NC-ND 4.0; P193 (bottom) Wiglaf, Wikipedia.co.uk; P194 British Library; P195 Edward Brooke-Hitching; P196 Metropolitan Museum of Art; P197 Ghent University Library; P198 Pvasiliadis / Wikipedia.co.uk; P199 Metropolitan Museum of Art; P200 (top) British Library; P201 British Library; P202 Yorck Project; P203 Cornell University Library; PP206-207 Rijksmuseum; P208 Gallerie dell'Accademia, Venice; PP210-211 Royal Museums of Fine Arts of Belgium, Brussels; PP214-215 Edward Brooke-Hitching; P216 (left) Wikipedia.co.uk, public domain; P218 Cornell University; P219 British Library; P220-221 Prado Museum; P222 Mauritshuis, The Hague; P223 British Library; P224 Beinecke Rare Book & Manuscript Library; P225 Barry Lawrence Ruderman Antique Maps; P226 Folger Shakespeare Library; P228 Folger Shakespeare Library; P229 Paul Hermans; P230 Yorck Project; P231 Barry Lawrence Ruderman Antique Maps; PP232-233 (both images) Getty Research Institute; P234 National Gallery of Art; P235 Wellcome Collection; PP236-237 Image courtesy of Boston Rare Maps, Southampton, Mass., USA and HS Rare Books, Buenos Aires, Argentina; P238 (top) Public domain; P238 (bottom) © OpenStreetMap contributors; P239 Public domain; P240 Library of Congress; P241 (top) Public domain; P241 (bottom) Library of Congress; P242 State Library of Pennsylvania; P243 Wellcome Collection; PP244-245 Met Museum.

Every effort has been made to find and credit the copyright holders of images in this book. We will be pleased to rectify any errors or omissions in future editions.

First published in Great Britain by Simon & Schuster UK Ltd, 2021
A CBS company

Editorial Director: Ian Marshall
Design: Keith Williams, sprout.uk.com
Project Editor: Laura Nickoll

1 3 5 7 9 10 8 6 4 2

Simon & Schuster UK Ltd
1st Floor
222 Gray's Inn Road
London WC1X 8HB

www.simonandschuster.co.uk

Simon & Schuster Australia,
Sydney

www.simonandschuster.com.au

Simon & Schuster India,
New Delhi

www.simonandschuster.co.in

A CIP catalogue record for this book is available from the British Library

Hardback ISBN: 978-1-3985-0355-7
Ebook ISBN: 978-1-3985-0356-4

Printed in Italy